METAPHORPHOSIS

Speaking in Tan(g)kas

A Joint Anthology from GMGA Publishing
and Pixel and Feather

Danny Gallardo | Author

Ayo Gutierrez and Dess Balota | Co-authors
Jinque RD | Artist

Foreword

By Antonello di Carlo

Italian Poet and Publisher

Words are the most important vehicle for our emotions. In pandemic we are experiencing, for most people, it is a period typical of waiting with suspended lives. Fortunately, this is not the case for those like us who write in verse. In fact, during this long period of lockdown, the writing did not stop. On the contrary, "our ink continued to flow copiously on our pages"

because we all know and share, for example:

- the many anti-Covid laws suppressed our freedoms;
- the impossibility of being able to meet family, friends
  and relatives;
- the changed habits of our daily lives; and
- the economy that is slowly crumbling because of the
effects
  of Covid-19.

We did not give up. With perhaps more significant deliberateness and courage than before this sneaky and invisible enemy arrived, we continued to write our poems, our sonnets, our madrigals, our haiku, our tankas. Also, we continued to create new forms of poetry, such as that contained in this extraordinary anthological collection titled *Metaphorphosis*. I am not an expert in English and all its facets that often depend on those who use this language to present their writings to the world, but I know poetry in all its nuances. Moreover, I am a lover and a lover of philology—studying languages—and philosophy.

Thanks to these ambitions, it was easy for me to reconstruct the etymological roots that lie behind the word metaphorphosis. It is the product of two words, which not by chance, have very ancient origins and are:

- The word metaphor in ancient Greek μεταφορά, means: "I transport". In contemporary linguistics, it is a figure of speech that implies a transfer of meaning. When the word occupies the place in the sentence, it gets replaced by another whose essence or function overlaps with that of the original term, thus creating images with a solid, expressive charge. We base the metaphor on a relationship of similarity between the starting term and the metaphorical term. Still, the evocative and communicative power of the metaphor is all the more remarkable; the more times we compose, the more distant the semantic field is.

In cognitive linguistics, we define the conceptual metaphor as one conceptual domain in terms of another, for example, one person's life experience versus another person's experience. The philosopher Aristotle himself, in his impressive work titled *Poetics*, defines metaphor as the transfer to a thing of a proper name of another or from genus to species or from species to genus or from species to species or by analogy.

- The word metamorphosis also comes from the ancient Greek μεταμόρφωσις and means transformation, change of shape or passage from one state to another. Here the semantics of the two words have married the purpose or, better said, the last aspect is inherent in the words themselves and metaphorphosis comes out, a compound word. I hope that whoever is reading this foreword will forgive me if perhaps I have been long-winded. Still, this clarification and etymological reconstruction was necessary to understand what we are talking about. Not all of us are poets, experts, and not all of us have had the pleasure of discovering and reading this new poetic genre. It was very easy for me to understand what lay hidden behind this sophisticated pun that readers will find not only as the title of a book, but soon, I am convinced that it will become a neologism or a synonym for the global world of poetry with which we will describe this fresh, interesting and new poetic form known as "tan(g)ka" invented by the brilliant Danny Gallardo. I am not fortunate enough to know Mr. Gallardo personally, nor, least of all, the other poets who took part in this project, but I believe that for a correct and objective foreword and review of this anthology, this can only be a positive element. It is easier for me to study and understand the *animus poeticus* I do not know personally by reading his or her verses. When you know someone, you can never be an objective observer and descriptor because there will always be subjective elements that will interfere and influence a correct analysis.

When my dear, esteemed poet and friend Ayo Gutierrez invited me to write the preface to this exciting anthology, I was happy to do so and even more curious to read it to learn about this new poetic experiment. I sincerely hope that it will soon become an integral part of the poetry world, along with sonnets and haiku. Her beautiful and ambitious initial project has now become a reality; and finally, the anthology we have all been waiting for is born. It contains poems by poets in English in a book addressed to all English-speaking peoples and published by GMGA Publishing. During this enjoyable reading, I took notes, underlined passages, and transcribed the verses that struck me most and that best present, and describe who wrote them.

I recognized and appreciated the importance and beauty of the editorial project, and this was one reason I agreed to write the preface.

I have read poems that do not need to be presented and argued such as the verses by **Danny Gallardo** in which the poet writes what he sees. That is nature and its elements that move, merge, and evolve, manifesting themselves more and more under different forms and more and more multiple dynamics. And here metaphor and metamorphosis become the rule and no longer the exception: they become metaphorphosis.

Continuing with the reading and here I am at the tan(g)ka by **Dess Balota,** who with discreet elegance with her metaphorphosis almost seems to worship nature religiously.

Reading the verses of **Ayo Gutierrez**, a poet whose style and virtue I know very well, and I see they trigger the fascinating mechanism of metaphorphosis differently; in fact very often with her it starts from the human being and remains in the human being and uses nature, the world and her life experiences as a choreography.

For **Rosario B. Villaluz** she expresses the metaphor and metamorphosis in what is the unknown which is perhaps frightening, but which one cannot do without.

The style of **Gingging Navarro-Laude** brings nature

back to the center of poetic reflection, but the human being always remains the principal actor of this inevitable symbiosis.

Ganesh Pradhan uses the themes of passion and love to develop his metaphorphosis. In the verses of this poet, nature moves and articulates itself around feelings.

We aim the poetics of his friend **Amit Shanckar** at describing the wonders of nature that return to interact with the human being and his emotions with a fantastic play of colors and metaphors. They create the evolutionary and dynamic presupposition of his metaphorphosis.

Ipsita Ganguli reports the object of her contemplation on love in the manner of the great Italian poet Dante Alighieri, in whom love is the most powerful geophysical force around which the entire universe moves and develops. Everything starts and ends with love.

In **Madylin de Leon**'s verses it is easy and beautiful to understand how her attention turns to the temporal aspect that the poet uses as a cage to trap surreal perceptions, idyllic moments and atmospheres that develop from dawn to dusk. If left free, she fears they may run away.

Nirupama Jayaram with firmness and resignation brings nature back to the center of the universe, and with it also the sensations it transmits and with which it interferes with the soul and heart.

Ernesto P. Santiago never openly touches on issues such as freedom and fundamental rights in his verses, but they remain the key to reading his poetics, made elegant also thanks to the correct use of metaphors that amplify its beauty and quality.

Barbara Ehrentreu and **Karina Guardiola-Lopez** fix on the transformation. Metamorphosis is the center of their reflections, the example of the caterpillar in the world of nature is perhaps the living creature that better defines the phenomenon between metamorphosis and metaphor. Equally pleasing is the example of a "word comprising only four syllables" that encompasses all the power of transformation and the very meaning of life. These two stupendous metaphors almost seem to ask a question: "Does the world change by itself or is it the change of the individual elements of nature that change the world?"

Martin Willitts Jr and his verses almost seem to caress the expectation of events and suggest to the human being to enjoy the small gifts that nature grants us every day, such as a sunset or the chirping of crickets.

Maria Evelyn Quilla-Soleta is the first poet who boldly describes the painful and grotesque but also indispensable metamorphosis for the human being and for the nature that surrounds us.

Baby Mayla brings to the center of her thoughts the figure of the grandmother that she uses as a beautiful metaphor between spirituality and nature, between prayers and phenomena, to describe where life began and how it will end.

Sam Higgins transforms his elegant metaphors and their always very appropriate use into the central fulcrum of his hermetic poetics, through which he lets his metaphorphosis filter.

Karyn Powers uses the metaphor of birds, their flight and migratory routes with great mastery of the subject and with light elegance to stigmatize the change of seasons, the passing of time and the very evolution of life.

With **Annette Wengert Tarpley**, her metaphor and transformation become almost a single moment of growth on which she articulates her poetics, always current and attentive. Her metaphorphosis has an evolutionary function and seems almost an opportunity with which to address sensitive issues of an ever-changing daily life.

We return to India and to poets such as **Jyoti Nair Vandana Sudhee**, **Srivalli Rekha Ankita Baheti**, **Mridusmita Choudhury**, **Aafiya Siddiqui**, **Karil Anand**, **Dipanjan Bhattacharje** and **Arundhati**

Mukherjee with whom the millenary philosophy and spirituality of India return to being with all their vehement source of inspiration, comparison and continuous search for answers that only nature with all its wonderful creatures, colors, scents, and peculiarities can give. Those answers that satisfy the poet who will find peace and balance thanks to it.

Now let's make a quick excursus into the North American school, starting with **Robert Hirschfield**. With this poet, spiritual love returns to occupy a central and indispensable role for his poetics and for the life that belongs to him. Love is a starting point and a point of arrival, but in this space-time interval, love will always be there, even if it has transformed or evolved.

Kathy Jo (Blake) Bryant attributes to music a cathartic power so powerful as to transform people and the very reality in which they live. All this happens because music has a therapeutic power not only towards human beings but also towards animals, plants, flowers and all the other single elements of nature.

Rebecca Lowe sees life and death as a single entity, in fact it almost seems that she has embraced the basic principles of modern chemistry on the one hand and Epicureanism on the other (Epicurus who taught that mental pleasure was the highest good). In this world nothing is created and nothing is destroyed but everything is transformed. For this reason, we must not see life and death as two different and antithetical moments. On the contrary, they are a single great moment that develops in a continuous metamorphosis that in her poetry Rebecca calls reincarnation.

Dennis Brown, perhaps among his compatriots, is the poet who talks about transformation without resorting to particular philosophical aspects. His point of observation is more experimental than ever. In fact, for this poet the metaphorphosis coincides with the transformation that all living beings have with conception, birth, growth and death, which are at the same time powerful metaphorical figures.

Andrea Lodge struck me for the way he uses the metaphorical figures and oxymorons that are the primary focus of his poetics and that accompany human existence from beginning to end not in a carpet of roses but through tortuous and complex paths such as it is life itself.

Rp Verlaine seems to write in his verses by using a camera. His poetry seems to comprise many frames through which the poet has masterfully captured the continuous metamorphosis of the society in which he lives.

Emily Reid Green gives a mystical, gentle, sometimes almost religious touch, in which she entrusted the cathartic power to prayer or, better said, to the need to take refuge in prayer, and in this placid articulation of words and metaphors, too. The sound of thunder can appear respectful and discreet.

With **Sharon Wagoner**, rebirth in other forms is the ultimate goal of true metamorphosis, and the important thing is to overcome this physical or metaphysical state. It reminds me a lot of Machiavelli's thought according to which "the end reached justifies the means that have been used" a bit like the constant exhortations made to the caterpillar that has become so used to living on the leaf that it is afraid when the time comes to turn into a beautiful chrysalis.

Joel Trevor Sauners and his poetics, through the use of sharp rhetorical tools, bring attention to the fact that life is a continuous transformation that is most often painful and never banal or predictable.

David Wagoner is one of the most original poets of this extraordinary anthology. The metaphor and metamorphosis are the supporting pillars of his poetics, but the human being must inevitably manage the latter, even if it must be a progressive evolution made up of small steps to be enjoyed and which are necessary to reach higher peaks.

The Pakistani poet **Sarfraz Ahmed** uses metaphors as necessary tools with which to achieve the metamorphosis necessary to pass from one state to another, but this step is never trivial or obvious but must have an almost epic flavor. Life is a set of encounters and clashes, just like a continuous battle in which the fight is more important and fulfilling than the victory itself.

Florabelle Lutchman and her poetics is made up of many neoclassical notes that revolve around the concepts of happiness, luck, and suffering. It is a sort of *Panta rei post-litteram* that is combined with the most modern philosophical concepts related to "becoming".

With **Imran Khan Bhayo** nature, its beauty, trees, plants, birds, the sky, the clouds and the thousand colors of the universe return with arrogance to be the central theme of the poetics of a man who uses metaphors as wonderful brushes to draw on a canvas called metamorphosis.

For **Andrew Geoffrey**, the world is a single space-time entity in which man, if he does not want to undergo the global transformation that is taking place, must confront it in continuous daily battles; but this metamorphosis, even if it is an enemy, remains indispensable as it is always the other side of the scale without which there would be no balance and harmony.

Anna Maria Dall'Olio and her tan(g)ka with a familiar flavor, through the use of refined metaphors, urges the human being to make the necessary change to achieve balance, peace and happiness. Sometimes the changes are so frightening that the human being prefers to live suspended in limbo just like that caterpillar that at some point would like to interrupt its metamorphosis because it is afraid of becoming a butterfly.

Sakina Mohammed writes verses full of a lot of spirituality, to which she approaches metaphors that bring nature back to its central role, nature and thus also the continuous metamorphosis which is sometimes painful but indispensable. In fact, not all buds will blossom and not all baby sea turtles will reach the ocean, but life, understood in its most global meaning, must continue thanks to cyclical transformations.

Amb Lovelyn P Eyo uses metaphors with the awareness that metamorphosis is necessary for the evolution of life, but the human being must face day after day the awareness that the fear and unknowns that the future holds often make us feel like a lion who discovers that he is not totally free in the savannah but that he lives in a natural reserve where there are other factors that will determine his change and his very existence.

We can express words in many languages, but by changing the language, the emotions do not change because if an author can describe his feelings with words, he or she will break down borders and travel all the ways in the world. In this period, poetry has a cathartic function, as it purifies the malaise given by the removal of affectivity... Looking at the beauty of life through the eyes of poets can only bring refreshment to the soul.

Writing is not a simple linguistic or stylistic exercise, but it must become an excellent intercultural bridge because we can only achieve true wealth through sharing and knowledge among peoples.

Only in this way can the word reach all places on earth, overcoming the highest mountains, the largest oceans, to be read by all. The poems can be more or less beautiful, but it is not the space-time location that decrees their evolution. Words, the real ones, those of the soul, have no time, no space because they carry the sense of memory and knowledge.

Poetry is a cure for the soul; it is the maximum capacity for dialogue, as the poet knows how to express his feelings by being able to make himself understood by other people. He is a bit like the musician who, with the help of notes, succeeds in composing pieces with which he expresses everything he cannot do through words. The poet performs the same actions. When inspiration comes, he or she weaves their wonderful tapestries using only "a blank sheet and a pen that do not need to be guided."

During these two years, because of the pandemic, many things have happened, and nothing remains the same. Every day always has something different from the previous one. However, the only thing that will never change in the universe is the function of poetry that existed, exists, and will always exist to comfort the hearts of millions of people. Then, this ambitious project called *Metaphorphosis* becomes a reality because "poets will never lay down their weapons," especially in moments like these. They know how to take each other by the hand and donate their talents, making them travel everywhere. The words of poets with this project will cross the world because the world is the home of poets.

INTRODUCTION

Danny Gallardo

Inventor of Tan(g)ka and Founder of Tan(g)ka Society

Everything is changing. The world has transformed from the rock age to other ages, and now to virtual age (time of internet). Even in poetry, there is change. It varied from romanticism to modernism. In the early twentieth century, from fixed pattern of rhyme and meter, Walt Whitman had shaken the poetry world and redefined poetry by introducing "free verse." A lot of variations mushroomed in our time (21st century). One of which is "visual poetry", popularized by Dr. Epitacio Tongohan (a.k.a. Doc Penpen Bugtong Takipsilim). Thus, he is considered and internationally acclaimed as the "Father of Visual Poetry." Another one is "hay(na)ku." Eileen Tabios, considered as one of the foremost Filipino-American poets of the 21st century, is revolutionizing it around the globe. And now, the epoch has come. I am introducing "tan(g)ka" to the world.

I created the "tan(g)ka", a variation from Japanese "tanka" whereby the poem's five lines are constrained by word count, instead of syllable count; one-word first line, two-word second line, three-word third line, four-word fourth line, and five-word fifth line. It can also be reversed, that means, the five-line verse may also have five words in the first line, four in the second line, three in the third line, two in the fourth line and one in the fifth line. To further differentiate "tan(g)ka" from "tanka", aside from syllabic count to word count:

"Tanka", a popular form of Japanese poetry is similar to "haiku" which has a structure of 5-7-5-7-7 (a total of 31 syllables) as compared to 5-7-5 (three-line verse of haiku). On the other hand, "tan(g)ka" is my innovation of "tanka" which is partly inspired by "hay(na)ku" of Eileen Tabios . "Hay(na)ku" is a tercet where the first line is one word, second line is two words, and the third line three words.

Here is Tabios' first "tan(g)ka" which is also a visual poem where the source-text is provided and its edits reveal the source-text (not included here) for the resulting "tan(g)ka":

Balikbayan

Tour
Archipelago where
Grandmother always grins
I forgot ground ever-shifting
Abandoning misery became concept: poem

Here is my "tan(g)ka" derived from source-text of Balikbayan by Tabios:

Poem
A concept

Abandoning misery ever-shifting
That grandmother always grins
Missing to tour the archipelago

Not only that, I also introduced in this book variations from "tan(g)ka". Some of which are:

"Tan(g)ka Sonnet" – created in two patterns:
            a.) tan(g)ka, couplet, tan(g)ka, couplet
                1-2-3-4-5, 5-5, 1-2-3-4-5, 5-5
            b.) tan(g)ka, tan(g)ka, quatrain
                1-2-3-4-5, 1-2-3-4-5, 5-5-5-5

"Abecedarian Tan(g)ka" where each word begins with each succeeding letter in the English alphabet.

I am thankful to my co-authors – Ayo Gutierrez, who challenged me to found the Tan(g)ka Society (a group of poets engaging in "tan(g)ka"), as well as for attracting foreign poets to write "tan(g)ka"; and to Desiree Balota who initiated this anthology to come into being. I am also grateful to the top-caliber (local and foreign) poets around the world who contributed their works to this book.

I hope this book will open the door to engage more people to write "tan(g)ka" and do their own variations out of it. Reading this book will inspire everyone to create new things to influence humanity and change the world.

Table of Contents

This section introduces you to the writings of the author and his co-authors. Gallardo, Balota and Gutierrez use the fundamental tenet of tan(g)ka and use it to expound on their chosen themes.

METAPHORPHOSIS

From intricate conversion of life
Two souls will unite
For point-blank transfiguration
Vivacious future
Kismet

Two
Lost souls
Espy their epiphany
And find the serendipity -.
The metaphor of life's metamorphosis

-Danny Gallardo

ON HOPEFIELD

when
you see
twilights as rosebuds
certain of dawns' blooms,
your thorned midnights will wither

even before the cocooned sunrise
butterflies onto day flowers
blossoming to bouquet
your rose-filled
noons.

-Dess Balota

ESSENCES

Tears
Marred spirit
Blood and swear
These are your insignias
What cuts deep builds fortitude

Every syllable of your sentence
Outburts beyond aesthetic beauty
We are bemused
You are
Uncontrived

-Ayo Gutierrez

Danny Gallardo | Philippines

DANNY GALLARDO is the founder of the Tan(g)ka Society and considered as 'Bard of the Beautiful' because his writing conveys beauty that leaves an indelible imprint on the heart and soul. He is the inventor of the tan(g)ka, his innovation from the Japanese form of poetry called *tanka*. The inspiration for the tan(g)ka comes from the *hay(na)ku* of Eileen Tabios, whom he convinced to write her first tan(g)ka poem. This prolific poet, who weaves lines of poems in his solitude, has inclined himself into his passion for writing in order to find the meaning of life. In his quest for truth, he came to a point that he has swum the depth of the sea of knowledge, unveiled the immensity of nothingness and searched relentlessly for better solutions and more explicit answers to the puzzle of life. According to him, poetry is the avenue of expression. In it, he can express himself. As a poet, he conveys subtlety with power. Hence, when he weaves lines, he writes from his heart.

This poet from Zambales is a Pentasi B awardee who has written and co-authored books like—*Bards from the Far East—Anthology of Haiku and Kindred Verses*, *Plethora of Poetry and Tanka and Tan(g)ka*. He still has books that are lined up and ready to be published. He is also a sonneteer and has written over 300 sonnets. When not writing, he paints using charcoal and watercolor.

TWILIGHT METAPHORPHOSIS

Union
Of two
Souls in motion
While beholders throw glimpses
To the metaphorphosis of nature.

The sun and the sea
In their evanescent intercourse
To create metamorphosis
In whole
World.

Where
The result –
Change comes suddenly
From postmeridian to night
Half the world in darkness.

Nature creates an aesthetic oeuvre –
Surroundings turn into twilight
When red sun
Plunges into
Sea-horizon.

World
Is watching
The romantic scene
Waiting for the climax
Of a pulchritudinous natural phenomenon.

AURORA METAPHORPHOSIS

Inveterate
Daily sighting
A natural proclivity
Rises in radiant east
Linchpin of all living things

Day is free from enubilous
Darkness, hence a pulchritudinous
Aura will come
Bright, new
Genesis

Alchemy
From dark
To effulgent light
Now a gezellig meliorism
Eve absquatulates little by little

And turns into ardent ataraxia
Creating a bucolic atmosphere
And have eudaimonia
To aphotic
Individuals

It

smiles as
To imbue positivity
Wherein beholders feel cynosure
And gives hope to everyone

The start of new day
From the melancholy night
And life's iniquity
There's hope
Aurora

ABECEDARIAN TAN(G)KA

After
Being born
Conceived from burning
Desire and being inspired
Extremely by power of pen

From
Great mind
Having the panorama
In wide multi-dimensional world
Just bestowed upon the poet

Knowing
Lots of
Mystery behind the
Nebula of poetic wisdom
Oozing from the profound thought

Painted
Quasi-masterpiece for
Rekindling love of
Sagacious poetry visually conveyed
To awaken, heal, inspire humanity

Unbosomed
V isual poetry
With abstract and
X-factor artistry of
Yuppifying and avant-garde magnum-opus
Zestful, aesthetic work of Art

LITERARY METAPHORPHOSIS
(a tan(g)ka with rhyme)

Being
From nothing
Can weave something
To create literary thing -
The metaphorphosis of creative writing.

Abyss
Mind plunges
Sea of wittiness
And in profound loneliness
Will express art of creativeness.

Idea
Begets panorama
From an iota
Will start a scintilla
To form a literary plethora.

Metamorphosis
Intellectual synopsis
Inner self changes
From the imaginative deepness
To form a literary bliss.

Emptiness
To fly
Sky of senses
And out of nothingness
One can create a masterpiece.

HOME

Adversary succumbs to this haven
No one can enter
Into this latibule
Which is
Home

Home
Can be
Heaven on earth
Where there is harmony
Among each other - halcyon family

BILINGUAL TAN(G)KA SONNETS

IRIS

Throw
A glimpse
The unforgettable occurrence
Ghosting in the iris
That always visits in dreams.

Insist
To ignore
But it persists
Like soul to free
From the bondage of imagination.

In the corner of thought
I am copulating with words
Flowery words to become oeuvre
To change the slumbering view

ALIKMATA

Tinapunan
Ng tanaw
Di malimutang pangyayari
Na nagmumulto sa alikmata
Paulit-ulit na dumadalaw sa panaginip.

Pinilit
Kong binalewala
Ngunit ito'y nagsusumiksik
Animo'y kaluluwang ibig lumaya
Mula sa bilangguan ng imahinasyon.

Sa isang sulok ng kaisipan
Kinakaulayaw ko ang mga salita
Mabubulaklak na salitang magiging obrang
Babago sa tulog na pananaw.

*pattern: tan(g)ka, tan(g)ka, quatrain
1-2-3-4-5, 1-2-3-4-5, 5-5-5-5

POETIC METAPHORPHOSIS

Empyreal
Motley rainbow
Beauty of words
In sky of thought
Nebulous wisdom in wide panorama

Poetry is metaphorphosis of wisdom
Created to change one's heart

Sky
The rendezvous
Of poetic words
Where thought is conceived
To pour inspired literary wisdom

Then rain of blessings showers
From the sky of poesy

MATULAING METAPHORPHOSIS

Malalangit
Bahagharing kulay
Yuming mga salita
Sa langit ng diwa
Karunungang maulap sa malawakang pananaw

Tula ay metaphorphosis ng karunungang
Nilikha upang baguhin ang puso

Langit
Tagpuan ng
Mga matulaing salita
Kung saan kaisipa'y ipinagbuntis
Upang magsaboy inspirasyong literaturang karunungan

Bubuhos ang ulan ng biyaya
Mula sa langit ng pagtula

*pattern: tan(g)ka, couplet, tan(g)ka, couplet
1-2-3-4-5, 5-5, 1-2-3-4-5, 5-5

PAMINGGALANG-BAYAN

Nagmula
Sa Maginhawa
Ngayon ay naglipana
Bawat panig ng bansa
Bayanihan - isang Filipino na kultura

Nakuha
Ang tema
Mula sa Bibliya
Sa Aklat ng Gawa -
Hingin pangangailangan, magbigay ng kaya

Nagpasimula
Si Patricia
Ng isang penomena
Ang pagtulong sa kapwa
Gagayahin ng ibang mga bansa

Pakukusa
Ang ipinapakita
Bayanihan ng masa
May dakila pa ba
Sa mga Filipinong sadyang nagkakaisa?

*Paminggalang-bayan - salin sa Filipino ng community pantry

*Patricia – si Ana Patricia Non, ang nagpasimula ng paminggalang-bayan (community pantry)

COMMUNITY PANTRY

Came
From Maginhawa
It's everywhere now
All over the country
Bayanihan - a culture of Filipinos

Got
The theme
From the bible--
The book of Acts:
Get need, give from ability
Started
By Patricia
Became a phenomenon
By helping the people...
This more nations will follow.

Initiative
Is shown.
Bayanihan: helpfulness, generosity
Is there indeed greater
From Filipinos who are united?

*Patricia - Ana Patricia Non, the one who put up the first community
pantry

A TAN(G)KA TRANSLATION TO "BRAKE"
BY LYK TAN

BRAKE
by Lyk Tan

Pause
Think twice
Left handed individual
Whenever you need, decide
Consider the shift of fate

Silently move a distance space
Freedom from deserved truth
Do not explain
Just move
Away

But
With poise
On whichever ground
Even doubting you pass
Stop with your left foot

Whenever in friction, give way
No one dies humble
Tiring and complaining
Maybe dainty
Heal

Expertly
Travel higher
Breathe another atmosphere
Practice post driving routine
Perspire and be a bee

PRENO

Hinto
Makalawang mag-isip
Kaliwete na indibidwal
Kung kailangan mo, magdesisyon
Kilalanin ang pagbabago ng tadhana

Payapang kumilos ang malayong puwang
Paglaya sa katotohanang dapat
Huwag nang magpaliwanag
Kumilos nang
Malayo

Ngunit
May tindig
Sa anumang tuntungan
Kahit nag-aalangang ika'y dadaan
Huminto sa iyong kaliwang paa

Anuman sa umpugan, magbigay daan
Walang namamatay na hamak
Napapagod at nagrereklamo
Maaaring delikado
Gumaling

Mahusay
Bumiyaheng mataas
Ibang kalawaka'y hingahin
Sanaying tapos pagmamanehong ruta
Magpapawis at maging isang bubuyog

(Salin sa Filipino ni Danny Gallardo mula sa
Tan(g)kang "Brake" ni Lyk Tan)

TAN(G)KA OUT OF TANKA

LITERARY GENESIS

TANKA

I plunge the abyss
Of the sea of wittiness
In my loneliness
Now I can freely express
The Art of creativeness

Inner self changes
Imaginative deepness
Metamorphoses
Intellectual synopsis
To form literary bliss

In my emptiness
I fly the sky of senses
For my genesis
And now, out of nothingness
I create my masterpiece

TAN(G)KA

Art
Of creativeness
In my loneliness
I plunge the abyss
Of the sea of wittiness

Metamorphosis
Intellectual synopsis
Inner self changes
Out of imaginative deepness
Will form a literary bliss

Genesis
From emptiness
Sky of senses
And out of nothingness
I create my beautiful masterpiece

BILINGUAL TAN(G)KA

1
Luha
Bumabalisbis sa
Salamin ng kaluluwa
Upang ilabas ang nadarama
Sa loob ng sugatang puso

Teardrops
Fall in
Mirror of soul
To release the feeling
Inside of a broken heart

2
Taludtod
Sadyang hinahabi
Ng humuhuning ideya
Sa langit ng diwa
Gamit ang malikhain kong kakayahan

Line
Being weaved
By whispering idea
In sky of thought
Using my deep aesthetic skill

3

Humahalimuyak
Kang bulaklak
Na sadyang namumukadkad
Sa hardin ng diwa
At sadyang nagpapatingkad sa buhay

Blossoming
Like flower
You're in bloom
In garden of thought
That gives color to life

4

Sumusugat
Ang alaala
Kapag may bumabalik
At sumasagi sa isip
Kaya't ibig ko nang lumimot

Wounding
The memory
One comes back
Touching in my thought
So, I want to forget

5
Naglulunoy
Sa laot –
Dagat ng diwa
Hayaang malunod nang kusa
Mapapait na nakaraang sadyang nagbabalik

Plunges
In offing –
Sea of thought
Allow to drown freely
Bitter memories are coming back

6
Tumatamis
Ang sandali
Ng iyong inspirasyon
Tumitingkad ang aking daigdig
Sa iyong wagas na pag-ibig

Sweetening
The time
Of your inspiration
Which brightens my world
By your love so pure

7

Kailan
Ko makakamit
Ang oong kaytamis
Damdamin ay sadyang nananabik
Paliguy-ligoy pa, di na makatiis

When
I'll attain
Your sweet yes
Feeling is so excited
Beating 'round bush, can't wait.

8

Buhay
Kung minsan
Ay walang bango
Tulad ng isang bulaklak
Naluluoy, lumalamlam, tigib ng siphayo

Life
At times
Is without scent
'Tis like a flower
Withering, fading, full of failure

9

Laot
Ng buhay
Kapag ito'y lalanguyin
Ay ibayong ingat dapat
Baka dalampasigan ay di marating

Offing
Of life
If to swim
One must be careful
Seashore will not be reached

10

Simsimin
Ang pait
Ng buhay dito
Sa mundo, subalit maghintay
May tamis, ngumingiting umaga'y darating

Savor
The bitterness
Of life here
On earth, but wait
Sweet, smiling morn will come

11

Mahuhuli
Din kita
Pinahirapan mo ako
Mailap, mabilis ayan na
Di ka na makawala – tutubi
I'll
Catch you
Though it's hard
You're elusive…swift…
Now you cannot escape – dragonfly

12

Pagdating
Isalubong mo
Ay ngiting kaytamis
Nang ang aking puso
Sa tuwa ay sadyang aawit

Welcome
Me with
A sweet smile
So that my heart
Will just sing in joy

13
Huwag
Mong dungisan
Ang iyong dangal
Kahit mahirap ang buhay
Mabuhay nang marangal at tapat

Do
Not blemish
Your honor, though
Life is so hard,
Live with integrity and rectitude

14
Paano
Ko mahanap
Ang iyong mali
Kung ikaw ay balatkayo
Nagtatago sa likod ng pagkukunwari

How
Can I
Find your fault
If you are fake,
You hide in a make-believe

15

Pasulyap-sulyap
Mga matang
Tumatapon sa iyo
Tapunan mo rin ako
Ng mga titig mong malalagkit

Glance,
Eyes that
Throw at you
And throw me too
With your so sticky eyes

16

Kumakatha
Ng makukulay
Na mga tayutay
Upang makabuo ng imaheng
Magpapaisip, magpapaukilkil sa diwa mo

Creating
These colorful
Figures of speech
To form an image
That will make you think.

Dess Balota | Philippines

Dess Balota surfs the wind on a paper plane wing when she closes her eyes to prepare the words she will place on sheets and screens. With degrees in education and literature, she's in for weekly drives for word shares and from time to time, sky and sea adventures for speech fests and write fests. She has won top prizes for poetry and impromptu speaking. Some of her poems have been published in anthologies, local newspapers, and literary magazines. She makes simple sandwiches and sketches leaves and marbles on random blank pages.

travel light

i
unpacked rivers
from zipped pockets
in my bloated backpack
then i walked on … floating …

downside up

sand
dissolved stones
into flowing boulders
and the waves hardened
into a ripple and sank.

sound asleep

when
i heard
my whisper resist
the holler of thunder,
lightning denied me a scream.

sweet beats

in
the quiet,
my fingers paradiddle
on milk candy bars
then roll on dark chocolate.

garden vows

and
tulips grew
from our rings
as we exchanged flowers—
white carnations and red roses.

rises

a
fallen star
in my basin!
as evening rain pours,
the fallen star grows...rises...

aha!

my
dry pond
bothers a familiar
stray cat. i show
my aquarium. the cat scampers.

unwither

morning
has bloomed
on the sidewalk.
cement has blossomed sunrises
to unwither my midnight feet.

(re)claim

water
stones roll
with dew pebbles
when wave rocks roll
onto shores of sand droplets.

distraught

driving
a car
on running water
overtaking and running over
flood running after dry ... drunken ...

expectant

my
guitar strings
are sterile clouds
ready to birth rain
on fingers pregnant with rainbows.

beyond titles

crown
and scepter
are king cobras
folded up in plastic,
sentenced by the deposed queen.

mutual conspiracy

the
sand castles
in my backyard
are your wind palaces
i built from my cornerstone.

rushed growth

a
brown leaf
glowed so i,
green in the wind,
pleaded for the sun's burn.

forethought

when
i saw
the rose bleed,
i knew the thorns
would swell into a wither.

revived

spent,
i plunged
into wells charged
for storing old sunrises
and rose dripping with fire.

hushed flows

let
the bandura
speak river flows . . .
i shall mute snares
for waves and water drums . . .

heeding

the
yellowing leaves
cry for dew.
the midnight rushes dawn.
the morning raises a green.

(s)hard(s)

buds
of dust
cinder-bloom from (a)shed
bouquets of flaming pebbles.
from garden (s)oil, (f)ire sprouts.

crossing

twilighting,
their sunset
cools the midday
scorching the noon bay ...
tonight, they shall sail ... rise ...

grace

when
You put
a star pebble
in my sand glove,
i regained my sun hand.

co-existence

the
cat drinks
from the pond.
the fish just swim
because the cat just drinks.

war

my
rag doll
stood up against
your tin soldier yesterday.
today, my rag doll is torn,

your tin soldier is broken,
and you play on
with rusty cans.
well then,
i ...

i
will sew
more rag dolls.
know that my fingers
are needles that never rust.

grow

when
the seedling
sealed the crack
on the stone wall,
i grew a flower box

from driveways and hollow blocks
broken from decade-old neglect.
the flower box
is now
home

to
the seedling.
sun rays seal
the stone wall now.
a few months from today,

the flower box will grow
into a prayer garden
that will bow
to the
wall.

it
will worship
the sun god
and grow light vines
that will reach the sun.

our secret (moon) song
[a tan(g)ka sonnet]

you
write me
verses of space
in my open drafts
so my sonnet could sing

our metaphors in moon couplets
chorusing the sunless yet bright,

gentle
yet bold . . .
i scribble moonshines
of breeze to embrace
your spaces. our pens duet

secret moonpaths as our ballpoints
epic-choir symphonies of Venuses . . . loving . . .

Ayo Gutierrez | Philippines

Ayo Gutierrez is an eight-time Amazon bestselling, multi-awarded author and international book coach. She has authored and co-authored poetry books including the titles, *Yearnings: Collected Poetry; Evocare: A Collection of Tanka, Chasing Zephyrs, Scentsibility* and *Chiaroscuro*. She also co-authored other bestselling motivational titles such as *Almost is the Same as Never, Chooseday: Life is a Matter of Choice, and Are You Ready: Timeless Principles and Proven Habits for Self-transformation.*

Her poetry has appeared in various international anthologies, e-zines, and literary journals.

She has successfully launched over 300 authors worldwide and continues to help others write and publish their books through her *Ink Your Legacy* Writing Courses and her online publishing platform, GMGA Publishing. Visit https://www.inkyourlegacy.com/enroll-here.html.

Burn

Heart
This most
Curious of instruments
Has me reeling madly
In your miscellany of talents

You have displayed much antics
To seduce my spirit
We fanned flames
Of our
Charades

I
Attempted to
Tame my desire
And followed your tracks
In a labyrinth of compromise

But I ache more deeply
When I see sparrows
Their silhouettes perching
Against my
Sunroof

Alas
The morning
Beckons them out
While I remain captive
In the confines of impossibility
There's no maiden to rescue
We take the blows
In the name
Of cruel
Love

Detachment

Silence
Ground zero
Blank space; vacuum
My thoughts float above
Feeling full amid my emptiness

Towards the center I dive
In sinking I recharge
Those scattered ideas
No longer
Present

Swift Detour

Stakes
Are high
In this trance
Passing through rabid dimensions
Meeting crosscurrents and whirlpools

The Pied Piper of Hearts
Revealed the sophisticated forks
Punctuated with cruising
On deadly
Waters

I
Instantly drowned
in the overflow
Of our diaphanous exchanges
Packaged in your costly meanderings

Stop!
I am
Out of control
My fabric unraveling fast
I cannot afford its luxury

Thankfully you are the first
To clutch the gear
And step hard
On the
Brakes

Filtration

In your soul-destroying craft
I had been manufactured
Into a counterfeit
Of useless
Bargains

Pride
Enfeebles you
In solitary confines
Oft attended by tears
A thorn in your flesh

These mad rush of sensations
Have galloped away. Fry
our magnetic fields!
Falsely labeled—
"Happiness"

You
Moved on
While I remained
Chained in the memories
Of muted embraces, stained confluences

With tinsel string and tassel
I waltzed my misery
Within the palace
Of poisonous
Verdigris

Lies
Artificially packaged
Embellished to perfection—
Pleasure but gilded brass
…I offered you a ruby

Give me back my wings
Surrender the Crown you
Hid far away
To hide
Me

Trapped
No more
Once I step
Outside your dwindling shadow
A new world opens up

Trees
Originally written as a black out poem
Source: National Geographic , April 2015 issue

One morning- a sweeping carnage
They were all dead
Dry and brown
Laced with
Destruction

Its
Telltale Story
Painted with rust
A troubling omen foretold
Leaving altered, irreversible ecosystems. Doomed.

GUEST AUTHORS

We proudly present the works of our 56 guest authors who were carefully selected from hundreds of entries worldwide for this anthology. This eclectic collection reveals the many and beautiful and sometimes poignant layers of "metaphorphosis" (metaphor + metamorphosis) as a theme.

when
words rain
as reserved storms,
drops of whispers speak
as pouring winds and whistles.

clouds clear...become verse-speech breaths
of voices: whispers, hollers,
captures, cares, charms
blowing...breathing...
pulsing...
-db

Rosario B. Villaluz | Philippines

Rosario B. Villaluz is a Certified Public Accountant. She co-authored *Semper Fi*, (Always Faithful) with her educator husband, Ivan Villaluz. *Semper Fi* is a collection of verses and poems about faith, hope, love and how these three values matter in the journey of life. While Rosario deals with local and international audits and Ivan endures the noise and laughter of his pupils in the exigency of their sworn duty for the State, the couple dabbles in poetry and free verse in between. Also, Rosario contributed her poems to *The Bards from the Far East: Anthology of Haikus and Kindred Verses* and *Scentsibility, Anthology* both under GMGA Publishing's banner. Along with other international authors, she also contributed poems to the anthology of Konect E-zine, *Rhapsodies, Volume I.*

It
Came like
A heinous thief
During one dark night
Even when doors were locked

All entry points duly secured
Yet, stealthily and forcefully
Smashing every thing
Obstructing its
Way

Panic
And fears
Enveloped the whole
Household of faithful servants
Defenseless of the ferocious attack

Unbeknownst to the trembling servants
Only One wasn't destroyed
The Crucifix hanging
On the
Door

And
The whole
Household rejoiced triumphantly
And they were totally
Rescued from harm and damnation!

Angel
Dewdrops
Crushed grass
Tiny worlds shimmered.
Before sunrise I grieved
A tired, withered angel lost.

Flightless, willingly she once embraced
Lullabies, sunshine, shadows, sorrow
Loved beyond sunsets.
Dawn's halo
Reclaimed.

Unfettered
She rose
Silent, she smiled
Reborn, spread her wings
Unseen, gently kissed me good-bye.

Now empty, the earth turns
Time on crippled hands
Rain anoints pain
Glitters, like
Dewdrops.

Gingging Navarro-Laude | Philippines

One could say that **Gingging Navarro-Laude** is a woman with a past.

She is a past Editor-in-Chief of the *Lex Obiter*, the official newsletter of the USC College of Law; the *Papyrus*, the newsletter of the USC College of Law Alumni Association; the *Tiara* (Queen City Toastmasters Club newsletter), and of the Philippine Toastmaster (District 75 newsletter), the last two both adjudged by Toastmasters International among the Top Ten Bulletins in the World.

After fulfilling her parents' dream of becoming a lawyer, she looked around and decided she wanted to fulfill her dream, too. She found her partner at Toastmasters International, married him, and gave up lawyering. With her husband's loving support, she is now a full-time nanny to their many cats and dogs. In her spare time, she scribbles, colors, reads, and, daydreams.

Angel

Dewdrops
Crushed grass
Tiny worlds shimmered.
Before sunrise I grieved
A tired, withered angel lost.

Flightless, willingly she once embraced
Lullabies, sunshine, shadows, sorrow
Loved beyond sunsets.
Dawn's halo
Reclaimed.

Unfettered
She rose
Silent, she smiled
Reborn, spread her wings
Unseen, gently kissed me goodbye.

Now empty, the earth turns
Time on crippled hands
Rain anoints pain
Glitters, like
Dewdrops

Ganesh Pradhan | India

Ganesh Pradhan is a high school boy and a budding young poet from India. He has a deep fascination for portraying his views and ideas as poetry. Ever since he started writing poems on online platforms, he has been published in one of the international anthologies titled *The Mirror* and in the Indian anthology titled *Blooming in the Moonlight*.

None but you.

Solely!
I walked-
Amidst the masses,
Saw and heard many;
Yet, I felt for none.

Many entwined hands and walked,
Perhaps with their parents,
kith and kin;
Friends or;
Lovers.

And!
I solely;
Watch them going-
For I hath none,
Ever since you have abandoned.

I vowed not to give
My hands, my heart,
To none howbeit-
I'm solely,
Yours.

None,
And never;
Could anyone win;
Or make me feel-
To Love as you did.

So I did not long,

For anyone after you,
If Not you;
Nor shall-
Be.

Amit Shankar | India

Amit Shankar is an advertising professional turned author. Currently based out of Gurgaon, Shankar has written five fiction titles and authored and edited two international poetry collections. His short stories have been adapted into films, plays, and skits.

Color me new

Bored
Of monochrome
The Moon revolts
Questioning natures' inherent diktat
Of constant change and evolution

Dreamy eyed, the ache intensifies
How would it look?
The golden glow
Moon wonders
Silently

Steal
Or borrow
From the Sun?
What if it refuses?
Delicately weighing the pros-cons

Why Sun, the Sirius quips
Vibrant palette simmers within
Of million hue
You need
Love

Hands
Treasuring, nourishing
The amber accentuates
Blushing Moon, coyly content
Basking in its real color

Ipsita Ganguli | India

A former hotelier, business consultant, author, travel writer, heritage enthusiast and poet, **Ipsita Ganguli** has worn, and continues to wear many hats, but above all, she has, and will always be a student of the myriad experiences that life holds out. Ipsita writes because she must. She has published her poems in several national and international e-zines and anthologies. She is also one of the leading characters in the poetry film, *Kolkata Cocktail*. Her solo compilation of poems *Of Love, Longing and Random Pondering* is available on Amazon.in and in select stores.

Love and Freedom

Love
befuddled me
That wondrous feeling
Evaporating into thin air
Pushing me into a vacuum

A terrifying feeling of emptiness
Engulfed my better senses
Waiting in anticipation
To embrace
Love

Yet
Love escaped
That elusive feeling
Played hide and seek
With my poor aching heart

Till I let love go
To its own fulfillment
As it should
Unchained existence
Freedom

Madilyn de Leon | USA

Also known by her pen name Soulhearts, **Madilyn de Leon**'s, love for the haiku started her writing journey. She writes mostly micro-poetry on love, pain, nature and emotions that touch the human spirit. Her poetry and photography are part of the published anthologies *Light Lines*, *Into the Void Arts and Literature Issue 2*, *Luminous Echoes*, *Stop the Stigma*, *A Poets Anthology* and *Yearnings*. You could read more of her poetry on her Facebook page, Instagram and Allpoetry.

Within

Sunrise
Golden yellow
Bounces off a mirror
Crystal clear, pear-shaped
Dewdrops fall from a leaf

Where the water shimmer silver
Clouds dance in seawater
Dipped in amber
Afternoon blush
Sunset

Seasons
Clock ticks
Day and night
Infinity locked with impermanence
In a meaningfully lived life

A wandering soul under moonlight
Walks on a journey
Slowly or hurriedly
To find
Beauty

Essence
Runs deep
In the heart
Of a searching man
What was lost was within

Nirupama Jayaram | India

Nirupama Jayaram writes under the pen name of njram6. She lives in the capital city of Chennai in the state of Tamil Nadu, India. She has contributed her works to several anthologies, and *Scentsibility* is her international anthology. She loves to pen poetry forms. Her favorite poem is "Ode to a Grecian Urn" by Keats. Her poetry book is due for release soon. Apart from that, she loves to cook and spend her time doing craft and art works.

Then an elegant autumn bird
Sung those winter songs
Fluttered with pride
Destination targeted
Sky

Wild
Seclusion alarmed
Sensing the fear
Drowning in cold abyss
Freezing in a vulnerable position

Lulling herself for eternal sleep
Onerous breath every time
Singes her pneuma
Permeating heart
Pain

Morose
Sorrow's showstopper
Waiting for warmth
Cuddling those salty droplets
Scars wrapping the nightmare thoughts

Shredding those decaying burdened feather
Learning to kiss solace
Adorning her self-esteem
Emerged chrysalis
Metamorphosis

Ernesto P. Santiago | Greece/Philippines

Ernesto P. Santiago spends all his free time between here and there, trying to learn something. He is too small for his ego. He is enough for himself. His verse has been widely published and has appeared in anthologies, in prints and online. He has authored two poetry books: *The Walking Man* (2007) and *The Poet Who Asked the Birds How To Fly* (2009). He was born in the Philippines. He lives in Greece, where he still continues to explore the poetic myth of his senses.

forces beyond i am

i
did it
before, so i
can do it again—
watching the sky that's uncopyrighted

letting the mind run freely,
daily moving forward, too—
a calm river
between two
mountains

going
to sea—
light and shadows,
i see only things
that directly motivate my soul

oh, look! a lone caterpillar
at the rainbow's end—
that world exactly
free as
butterfly

ah,
like dew
to green grass
i celebrate this beautiful
life, predetermined by the Unseen

Barbara Ehrentreu | USA

Barbara Ehrentreu is a retired teacher and tutor with two published novels, *If I Could Be Like Jennifer Taylor* and *After* and two poetry books: *You'll Probably Forget Me: Living With and Without Hal* and *The Child Poet: A Poetic Galaxy for Children*. She has written an award-winning screenplay, *The Kiss,* and is published in several anthologies including *Crossroads: A Poet's Life Journey* and Walt Whitman's Bicentennial Anthology, *Poets to Come*. Her work appears in several places, including on Norwalk Library's Poetry Page. She has received the Indian Independence Day Award given to only 350 people in the world, the Cesar Vallejo Award from Hispano Mundial Escritores, the Kairat Dussenov Parman Award and many others.

Transformation

Caterpillar
Crawls along
The green leaf
Looking for a place
To spin its silky cocoon

Tired and sleeping at peace
In gossamer strands of
Delicate white threads
It rests
Alone

Solitary
Its body
Undergoes a change
So drastic it requires
Many days to create it

One day it emerges from
Its covering and unfolds
Spectacular multicolored wings
Shining in
Sunlight

Surely
Such a
Transformation makes one
Believe in the miracle
Of God's majesty and power

Martin Willitts Jr | USA

Martin Willitts Jr, a Comstock *Review* editor, has twenty-five chapbooks including the Turtle Island Quarterly Editor's Choice Award, *The Wire Fence Holding Back the World* (Flowstone Press, 2017), plus twenty-one full-length collections including the Blue Light Award 2019, *The Temporary World*. His forthcoming book is *Harvest Time* (Deerbrook Press, 2021).

Shaking Sky's Tin Sheets

Rain—
unsettle uncertain
what today brings—
not one song complete,
no music, no love, nothing.

I pick up the fractured notes
crumbling night into dusk
throbbing tiny violins
interpreting heat—
crickets.

It
rains daffodils
mumbling their regrets
in spring, bringing promises
tomorrow will be cats and dogs.

My parent flatlines, shadow gone,
a quiet storm quickening,
touches piano keys
making light
rain.

Karina Guardiola-Lopez | USA

Karina Guardiola-Lopez is a writer, poet, actor, and educator from New York City. She has been published in various magazines, anthologies, and websites including For Women Who Roar, Writing For Peace, Great Weather for Media, The Scrib Arts Journal, Indolent Books, Poetica Magazine, Acentos Review, Latinoauthor.com just to name a few. She has also featured at various venues including The NYC Poetry Festival at Governor's Island, National Black Theatre, Bowery Poetry Club, Nuyorican Poets Cafe, Q-Boro Lit Crawl, The Bronx Museum, and many other locations. She has facilitated many poetry workshops such as Pens, Pads and Poets, B.A.R.S, American Sign Language, and more, for both youth and adults. For more information, visit www.kglopez.com

Publisher's Note: Karina's poem has been accepted on the merit of adhering to the theme "Metaphorphosis".

A Transformation 4 Two

Perception: Strangers

That four-letter word
That changes our lives so much
Some say it is love
Others will say it is hate
Either way, they're right

Phases: Getting to Know You

Waxing and waning
Alone among company
Mood swings and phases
You are both light and darkness
Reminding me of the moon

Persistence: Making this Work

With all your baggage
These strong arms are for lifting
Solid, soiled and sour
Accepting all of your parts
It's difficult to let go

Reconciliation: Lovers
We fight and we love
Will you paint me with your tongue?
Blend me with brush strokes
I will guide you without light
I too am a starry night

Maria Evelyn Quilla- Soleta | Philippines

Maria Evelyn Quilla-Soleta, or 'Eve' to many, is the bestselling author of *Finding My Heart*. She gives thanks to poetry. Her poems and stories are unadorned yet truthful, purposely warm and witty. People, things, living and non-living creatures, and even circumstances are subjects that inspire and give colors to her rhythms and rhymes, stanzas and lines. They give vibrancy and feelings to the words she pens. These feelings come to her in the stillness of the deep, quiet moments when she can commune with Him for inspiration and life. Evelyn's first love is writing, when, at six, she wrote her first poem in a school paper. In college, her forte was writing feature articles, personality sketches, and poetry. She was a freelance writer for local women's magazines before publishing her first book on poetry titled *My Twenty Poems*.

Motherhood is a subject close to her heart, and it inspires her to write. She has a keen eye and ear for the peculiar and mundane details of everyday life, endearing, in her lack of pretentiousness among the trivial and ordinary matters around her. Evelyn's four girls and beautiful granddaughter, Tala (with another one on the way), are her inspiration to pursue this first love of hers, ***Writing!***

DRIFTWOOD

Driftwood.
Brought home
By my Giadon
From her school fieldtrip
In Tagaytay Park and Zoo.

I thought some thorough cleaning,
Sanding, varnishing will brazen
This lowly 'animal',
Transforming it

Anew!

This
Grotesque figure
Will brave the
Painful grinding, peeling, scraping
But will turn out New!

Nothing could be truer than
For ALL of us
To go through
Refiner Fire's
Spews!

But
Through all
The deep scratches
Permanently scarred by others
Become the beautiful driftwood—You!

BABY MAYLA

Grandma's
Petitioning, imploring
Praying that everyday
You hold on resolutely,
Determined until May's perfect day!

Warmly-wrapped in your Mom's womb,
In moonbeams of yellow,
Stardusts of gold
Beautifully, you
Grow.

Waiting.
Eagerly wanting.
Grandest day coming!
Then we'll all hail
To a sweet, Godly thanksgiving!

Mayla is Excitement! She's Joy!
She's far beyond Love
Her parents' priceless
Doll to
Enjoy.

Theory?
Life's hypothesis?
Dear Baby Mayla—
You're God's heavenly gift,
Our world's most darling metamorphosis!

Sam Higgins | UK

An opportunistic writer based in Hampshire, UK, Sam Higgins finds escape in writing during stolen moments while his baby daughter sleeps, having recently discovered poetry as a way to digest the emotional complexities of fatherhood.

After

Yesterday, the earth reclaimed her
Amidst splintering stone and
Echoes of joy;
Sullen, silent,
Lost.

Pages –
Once threadbare –
With vivid inks,
Eminent from subtle pen,
She'd adorned with vibrant life.

Now entombed, encrusted by grief,
What becomes of us?
Colours fading, encaged,
But – wait …

Transcendence.
Footprints –
Shadows, apparitions,
Reborn in another:
Our daughter's soulful song,
The reasons I drink tea.

Ripples of a selfless life
Unearth vibrant, hopeful hearts,
Weather granite husks;
Whispering, bittersweet:
"Live".

Karyn Powers | USA

Karyn Powers writes poetry and flash-fiction. Her work has appeared in *Writers Digest: Show Us Your Shorts, Poems from Farmers Valley, Mush, Red Cedar*, and *Hummingbird literary magazines*. She is a member of the Wisconsin Fellowship of Poets, and is a contributing editor to *Wisconsin Central Time News*.

Thrum

thrum
wings beat
lifting in flight
frightened from close by
into bright white winter's light

I jerk back from it
too close too fast
with a start
two hearts
thrum

thrum
in space
waiting for breath
watching the bird fly
into the aquamarine afternoon sky

The Cleansing Rain

The rhythm of the Rain
Cleanses my inner soul
Behold the power
As rain
Purifies

Annette (Wengert) Tarpley | USA

Annette Wengert Tarpley hails from the United States and has won many awards and accolades from her poetry. Annette has many poems published online, her own play list of recitations, and performs recitations for other poets on YouTube produced by Sparrow Poems. She appears in many anthologies. Annette has published her first book *Poetry Potpourri*, and co-authored, *Uplifting, Poems of Positivity*, available on Amazon, and co-authoed a bestselling book *Two Hearts: A Poetry Collection*, with Sarfraz Ahmed. Annette is the administrator and the founder/administrator of the Facebook site, The Passion of Poetry.

Her Rebirth

Broken
Not defeated
Gaining inner strength
Momentum building to climax
Rebirth of her former self

Everything is possible within reach
Her energy is contagious
Her love abounds
Ever present
Everyday

Strong
Strengths unveiled
Embraced herself thoroughly
She accepted herself wholly
She learned to love herself

The beauty she finally found
In the freedom gained
Taste of independence
Purest joy
Elation

Onward
Blazing trails
A newfound life
Loving herself and life
Embracing the nuances of being

Her future was now defined
Her path now paved
She would embrace
Arms open
Herself

Jyoti Nair | India

Jyoti Nair is a quintessential Learning and Development / Project Management Professional. Presently, she works for a top-notch Indian MNC as the Capability Development Manager for multiple HR Business Units, where she partners to foster and speed-up transformation momentum for Center of Excellence (COE). She has won several accolades for her literary pursuits; she believes in incessantly whetting her writing skills, and traversing new learning bends each day. Way forward, she aims to harness the power of her pen, championing for the eradication of social stigma around mental illness, for the upliftment of victims of domestic violence and for curbing blatant incidents of child abuse.

Bodhi Blossoms

feuille-morte doesn't imply a manacle
shimmery soothing subtle clasp
mutation drizzling canopy
reddish-brown mettle
sepia

chrysalis
awakening mirths
bohemian azure ambles
butterflies drenched in jouissance
each twilight, a swooning cosmos

nonchalance: life's rule of thumb
our visions hung precariously
waning and waxing
ubiquitous garb
existentialism

universe hops into a carousel
seasons shuffle, seasonings simmer
transmutation in tow
beaming alchemy
recherche

Robert Hirschfield | USA

Robert Hirschfield is very much influenced by tanka. His work has appeared in Noon (Japan), Bear Creek Haiku journal (US), Ink Sweat & Tears (UK), and many other publications.

Publisher's Note: Robert's poem has been accepted on the merit of adhering to the theme "Metaphorphosis".

After Love

for *Julia*

After love
nothing moves

but time
backwards

a face
its green dart

of snow
your seventy-seven

years
blink

Rebecca Lowe | USA

Rebecca Lowe is a journalist, poet, performer and co-organiser of Talisman Spoken Word open mic and Talisman Zine. Her poem 'Tick Tick' won the Bread and Roses 2020 Spoken Word Performance award. She has had her poetry featured on *Radio 4's* Poetry Workshop and one of her poems was set to music as part of a choral series broadcast on *Radio 3*. Her first poetry collection *Blood and Water* is published by The Seventh Quarry Press. A further collection *Our Father Eclipse* is due for publication with Culture Matters in April 2021. She is on Twitter as @BeckyLowePoet.

Reincarnation

Dead?
Not quite –
A fresh song
Rises within every branch,
Bursting buds into new lives

I have been many things:
Once, a butterfly dancing
Wreaths of roses
Whispered love's
Demise

Spirals,
Dizzying stars,
Once, I sang,
And all the planets
Joined in perpetual whirling motion

I have cried Autumn's skies,
Bled red-veined leaves,
Conquered countless dawns,
Surging forth,
Alive

Changed,
Yet surviving,
Pulsing new shoots,
Even when darkness prevails,
Finding new ways of rising.

Dennis Brown | USA

Dennis Brown lives in the United States, residing in the state of Michigan. He is an educator with a degree in English Language and Literature. Dennis is married to Melissa and is the proud parent of two children, Meghan and Mason. He is a passionate writer with a focus on poetry. Dennis has collaborated with artists and poets alike, and has been recognized for his writing worldwide. He has received numerous accolades and has produced both commissioned and published work.

A Heart Transformed

A
Bleeding heart,
Filled with desire,
To chase true love,
In a world among strangers.

Within the hearts' red walls,
The arrangement of beats,
Enveloped in loneliness,
Echo throughout,
Unnoticed

A
Compassionate healer,
Hears lonely beats,
Pumping sound into chambers,
In a transformation of sorts.

A heart on the mend,
A Healing now within,
Touched from without,
Reversing course,
Repairing

A
healed heart,
Now forever touched,
Has found true love,
In a world among strangers.

A Transformation of Life

Infancy,
Child born,
A new beginning,
Full of boundless energy,
Ready to embrace the world.

Prepared to take a risk
To search for self-identify.
A sexual revelation
Of empowerment.
Adolescence

Adulthood,
Life awaits,
Into the world,
A child now released,
Ready to spread his wings.

Gray within his aging brow,
Wrinkles upon his face.
End is near,
Shallow breaths,
Death

Andrea Lodge | USA

Andrea Lodge is the author of Manic Marigold. She resides in Philadelphia with her husband and two disabled cats; Budgie, with only three legs, no tail, constantly drooling, and Loki, AKA Poki, AKA, Pokapotamus (because he weighs 20 pounds), a Scottish fold with only one folded ear. She studied English/Secondary Education at Holy Family University and taught middle and high school Writing and Literature after graduating. She is now a full-time writer and something resembling an artist. She has had several poems featured on Spillwords, two pieces included in an anthology by Havik, several poems and some prose in different issues of Alien Buddha Press' *Feminist Agenda, The Alien Buddha's Block Party: Blackout Poetry*, Alien Buddha's *Zine #12* and Alien Buddha's Zine #21, her poem, "Screaming at Tiffany's" was in the 12th issue of Voice of Eve magazine. She has also had some work featured in Danse Macabre's Entrée DM 123 and DM 125: Fete de Noel. She has also been featured in the Winter edition of Soul Lit's online zine, 2019. As of late, Andrea has written reviews for the books *Evocare* (Ayo Gutierrez, Eileen Tabios, Brian Cain Aene) and *The Tears I Never Told You* (JinQue RD). Andrea has also edited *The Tears I Never Told You* and *Are You Ready?* (Ayo Gutierrez, Gigi D. Sunga, Ph.D.) She has most recently had her poetry featured in the anthology, *Scentsibility,* a book of poetry related to the senses.

Untitled

Darkness
Of the
Blue night sky
Hides away the blackness
Like periwinkle on the sea.

Moon dancing across your lips.
I wanna kiss you
Every single second
Of every
Day.

Here
We are
Two twinkling stars.
We are the headlights
On foggy twisting mountain roads.

We are wraiths in forests
Shade souls in disguise
The decoy shadows
Hiding ourselves
Always.

Vandana Sudheesh | India

Vandana Sudheesh, a poet with a diverse voice, was born in Kozhikode district in the southern Indian state of Kerala. The UHE (Union Hispanomundial De Escritores) conferred her with the Cesar Vallejo World Award for Excellence in a Literary Field in 2020, in Spanish. She also received the World Poetry Prize Award (1st place from the Asian continent) for a posthumous tribute to the great poet Kairat Duessinov Parman, founding President of WNWU (World Nations Writers Union). She is a moderator of Motivational Strips and directs Asian writers through a parliamentary committee of forum members. Considering her passion, enthusiasm and contribution to world literature, she received membership in the World Nation Writers Union (WNWU). She is the anchor of "Mighty Quills of MS" from Motivational Strips. She published her first solo book, *The Humble Wrath* in August 2020. Her poems have been published in many magazines.

WITH APLOMB

Pyramids
Of love
Cascading with peace
Resurrection entwined in collision
With the desire to fly

Perceptions disregarded with no respect
To those words flippant
Rupturing the time
Of rise
Incessantly

Swirling was my heartfelt projections
Pioneering the redundant waves
With flames rising
Predicting souls
Unanimously

Stringent
Frivolous laces
Battered with thoughts
Unspoken and unflavoured within
To strengthen humanity and peace

Let each step taken forward
With gratitude as attitude
Be with aplomb
To undress
Audaciously

Sarfraz Ahmed | UK

Sarfraz Ahmed lives and works in East Midlands, UK, and is a careers adviser, branching out as trainer, assessor, and a careers writer. He has been writing poetry for over eighteen years and has contributed to many anthologies, including *Paint the Sky with Stars*, published by Re-invention UK, and many others published by the United Press, and many online contributions. His published books include his poetry debut, *Eighty-Four Pins* (June 2020) and *My Teachers an Alien!* (November 2020) which is a children's book with illustrator Natasha Adams. Green Cat Books published both books https://green cat.co/books. He has published his second collection of poetry, with co-author Annette Tarpley, *Two Hearts* (February2021). Sarfraz moderates the large Passion of Poetry group on Facebook and has a following on Facebook and Instagram. We can find him at open mic events. He has shared his poetry globally, including on the New York circuit.

Phoenix Breaks Free

Phoenix,
Breaks free,
From the chrysalis,
Flying through the fire,
Tastes freedom in his desire,

Mystical dragon going to war,
Gets ready to fight,
Pushes the boundaries,
With resistance,
Conquered

Fortitude,
Fly's high,
Once again free,
From all the chains,
Breaks free from the pain.

Beautifully Reconstructed

Make-up,
So precise,
Such intricate design,
Each color placed upon,
Pallet overflowing in full bloom,

As he enters the room,
He lights it up,
Like spring time,
So fine,
Masterful,

Presence
Beautifully reconstructed,
That she dominates,
Upon the dance floor,
The alpha male is no more.

Denia A. Claret | Philippines

DENIA A. CLARET is the publisher, visual artist and writer at Seven Rays Publishing through which she publishes the social studies (Makabayan-SIM) atlas, a multilevel supplementary— instructional reference and activities material with geography as an integrating unit for all primary education grades and high schools. Five thousand schools from the Department of Education nationwide sponsored by Agencia Espanola Cooperacion International have used this program since its launching in 2000.

Untitled

Equilibrium
Divine Innocence
Secret of transfiguration
Rise from human conditions
Hierarchy, being human, being divine.

Building for myself a Sanctuary
Sharing my own brightness
Vast and infinite
Loving-kindness
Transcendence.

Consciousness
Self-existence
Internal and external
Beyond five physical senses
Most Mystical aspect of Life.

Universal light of the cosmos
Transcending to solar system
Gaia's Star-born seeds
Star Beings
Stargazers.

Brain's most powerful in existence
Phenomena in modern science
Mind over matter
Placebo effect
Miracle.

Ivhee Tan Dinoso | Philippines

Ivhee Tan Dinoso is an AB Psychology graduate at De La Salle University–Dasmarinas. She worked as an HR Manager and Personnel Manager in resorts in the Maldives from 2015 to 2019. She also worked at PESO (Philippine Employment Services Office), Province of Zambales, and was a College Instructor at Lyceum in Western Luzon. This poet who is fluent in and understands eight languages was a former Filipino literary writer of the *Heraldo Filipino* of De La Salle University, Dasmariñas, Wistron InfoComm *Fresh News* (13 corporate sites communications writer) and writer/contributor to *Zambale News*. She is currently the HR Manager and Instructor at MACSAT.

MURANG BAGWIS

Bang!
Banayad pagputok
Baril ng gerilyang
Bagot lamang sa pandemya
Buwis bala ang malamyang taktika

Palipat-lipat ng pakpak, may pagkalito
Tuliro, mabilis na pumagaspas
Naumpog sa poste
Manlamlam agad
Laglag

Damo
Sa lupa
Siya ang nagpahimlay
Sa may tabing kalasada
Hinihipan ng malamig na hangin

Matalim na titig ng minanang mata
Di napupuwing kung humahanga
Sing taas paglipad
Babagsakan din
Lupa

Ipikit
Oo ipinid
Pilikmata, balintataw, alikmata
Nakakahilong masakit na sugat
Palaypay mong napilay, nangalay, bumigay.

NEOPHYTE WING

Bang!
Slow shot
Gun of guerilla
Boring only in pandemic
Risked bullet the clumsy tactic

Changing of wings, there's confusion
Puzzled, flapped wing fast
Bumped at post
Immediately fainted
Fell

Grass
In soil
It lets lay
Near by the street
Blowing by the cold air

Sharp glimpse of inherited eye
No mote when admiring
Flies so high
Falls to
Earth

Close
Yes, close
Eyelashes, pupil, iris
Dizzying, the painful wound
Your broken wing, sprained, succumbed.

.

Janna Therese Uy | Philippines

Janna Therese Uy is a poet, video editor, and owner of the WordPress poetry blog, *Save The Dreamer* since 2011. When not writing, she can be found watching video essays on YouTube, playing video games, and hunting for restaurants that are best for midnight snack runs. She was born in Manila and currently resides in Taguig with her sister, her best friend, and her dog.

An Afternoon of Jeans Hunting

Plus;
siXXXXXX L,
women's section limited,
BIG girls' corner joint
tucked away as eye sore.

Stiff mall is squared enough,
from local-fit acceptable;
Large. Medium. Small.
Extra Small.
Free-

Sized.
And when
I reveal you-
how foreign those mannequins
zeroed in my overflowing bigness,

rigid tiles flattered courage; ENORMOUS.
My steps sprung roars.
A Colossus awakened.
Holding space,
defiantly.

Srivalli Rekha | India

An MBA graduate, **Srivalli Rekha** also has an MA in English Literature. She loves to write, blog, and cook, take pictures, draw, and craft silly things. Nature is her greatest inspiration. Books and music are her favorite companions. She is a book reviewer at NetGalley, BookSirens, and The Writers Workout.

Her works have been a part of several anthologies (ebooks and paperback publications). She and four of her writer friends founded The Hive, a non-traditional publishing collective. They have published three anthologies and one minitales bundle as ebooks on Amazon and are working on the fourth anthology, set for release in Feb 2021.

Violets in Hand and *The House of Justice*, her self-published ebooks are available on Amazon. Her collection of micro-fiction is soon to be released as an ebook on Amazon KDP.

I'm the Same

You seem different, they say
Is it I wonder
Hiding a smile
They hesitate
Nod

Well
I shrug
Walking away as
Memories from the past
Play again in my mind

Yes, of course, why not
Anytime, anything for you
I'll be here
To help
Always

Yet
None reciprocated
My selfless efforts
When I was tired
Of being the support system

I'm still the strong one
Just careful, cautious, sensible
About my energy;
It's new
Me

Angel Mae Villarino | Philippines

Angel Mae Villarino is a 19-year-old girl who lives in Cebu. With her pursuit of growth and achievement in her writing endeavors, both in technical and creative writing, she is currently doing a Bachelor of Arts degree in Communication at the University of the Philippines in Cebu. She believes that art is an eye that when scrutinized closely, unravels the societal issues that not only women face but also the marginalized Filipinos, which reflects in the poems she writes.

She engages herself with organizations such as Tinta–UP Cebu, Flesh and Blood Artist Collective, and Istilo Poetry Cebu. Flesh and Blood's December collection entitled, "Lamang Lupa" which tackles the struggles of the LGBTQ+ people included her published poems "Cupboard Cell," and "Witches Don't Burn on This One"; and Katipunan ng mga Pluma chose her poem "Light in Hiding" to be included in their ebook anthology *"Aid from Art"*, which they themselves produced to raise funds for Filipino typhoon victims last December 2020.

Butterfly Cycle

Leaves
Have grown—
Just as how
Tiredness grows inside photosynthesis,
When greeneries were all eaten.

They were our towns, grounds,
And supper viands, but
We were fiends
They hanged
Upside-down.

Witches
In trials
We were considered—
Howbeit, absence of fire,
They still burned us alive.

Burning, exist not for light,
But also, for darkness.
Pushing us to
Open claustrophobic
Cells.

Unexpectedly,
We're fearless
Although grounds shake;
We now don't crawl
Brawls, but flap towards them

Dr. Lester N. Linsangan | Philippines

Lester N. Linsangan is an advocate of education and youth empowerment. He graduated with a Bachelor of Secondary Education degree from the Nueva Ecija University of Science and Technology, and during this time, he got the highest mark of 99% in a final teaching demonstration. He earned his Master of Arts degree in Education at the College of the Immaculate Conception (with academic citation); he got his 4-year course in ecclesiastical education at Institute of Religion; and finished his Doctor of Education major in Educational Management at Wesleyan University-Philippines (Cum Laude).

He is a former Division Head of the NEUST-Training Department; International Organization for Standardization University Internal Auditor; Adviser of different political and non-political student organizations.

He presented and published research papers both in local and International research journals.

He served as one of the authors of the Amazon bestselling book titled *Scentsibility*, along with award-winning, renowned, and prolific writers around the globe.

At present, he is teaching at NEUST and the Institute of Religion; he is a writer/author at GMGA Publishing; and coordinator of Office of Student Organizations, Activities and Development.

Dr. Linsangan is a proud mentee of Ms. Ayo Gutierrez.

Stupendous

Life
Is belligerent
It seems haunting
The wildest enviable stars
In the deep blue sea

Adding fuel to the fire
Makes the whirlwind upsurge
Plateful laughing stock
Is absurd
Unpardonable

Impediment
In speech
Is vocalizing fear
Echoing roar of beasts
And deafening silence of Seraphim

Love how it's being revamped
Philosophical style in verbosity
Is spontaneously spoken
Technically written
Intelligible

Howler
Is avowed
Enemy of transformation
Live unheard life remarkably
Death and change are inevitable

Glimpse in Disguise

Pinpricked
Colored papers
Flammable fancy wall
Fueled by futile process
Chirography speaks for you all

Even small circles do big
Glasses have clear flecks
And stipple with
Original pigmentation
Naked

If
Bright stars
Will fall down
The universe will decide
You have sunset or sunrise

Ankita Baheti | India

Ankita Baheti was born on 15 September 1986, in India. She has a Bachelor of Engineering (Hons) and was a meritorious student throughout her life. She worked as an assistant professor in college. After she married, she worked as technical content developer for a company in Gurugram. Then she moved to Qatar as a freelance worker. She was inclined towards poetry and article writing from her childhood. She likes to write about nature, feminism, and social issues. She is a co-author in an anthology named *Audacity of the Blank Page: Fight Against Lonliness, Women we know, Psithurism* in English and Mimansa, *Kavyavandi* part1, *Strotam* in Hindi. Currently, she is a full-time mother, taking tuitions and trying to contribute to society through her strong message bearing poems and articles.

Revolution 2020

Pandemic
Altered world
Economies went down
People lost lives unduly
Chaos took place all around

But it brought drastic revolution
Family time spent together
Value of virtues
Memoirs created
Corona

Envision
Enlightenment progressed
New things relearnt
Self-sufficiency new motto
Work started with widespread internet

Environmentalists happy, nature regained serenity
Care must, told clearly
Else suffer loss
Destruction massive
Fall

Pivotal
To ascertain
Role of individual
Essentially important for everyone
Help humanity grow, positivity flow.

Christine Marie Lim Magpile | Philippines

Christine Marie Lim Magpile graduated Cum Laude from the University of Santo Tomas and finished a Bachelor of Science in Secondary Education (B.S.Ed.) with a major in History. Currently, she works as a copy editor for the UP Press.

Apart from being a teacher and freelance textbook editor, she is also a textbook author for Basic Education (*Bayan Kong Pilipinas* 6, UPFA: 2010; *Media and Information Literacy*, Inteligente Publishing House: 2016; and *Filipino: Pagbasa at Pagsulat Tungo sa Pananaliksik*, Inteligente Publishing House: 2016).

Her haikus are included in the anthology, *Sustaining the Archipelago: An Anthology of Philippine Ecopoetry* (UST Publishing House, 2018). Her creative nonfiction "SM-Stop and Shop!" appears in the *4th UP Likhaan Journal*. Her flash fiction "Spoilers" appears in *A Treat of 100 Short Stories* (Anvil Publishing, 2011).

The Pianist

The grand piano felt proud,
As the pianist played.
A dynamic pair,
Delightful music.
Bravo!

Fingers dancing on piano keys.
Notes transformed melodic memories.
You're a prodigy.
Audience enthralled.
Encore.

Brilliant,
Like Mozart.
The sonata soared.
Music moved the audience.
Another concert awaits. Maestro prepares.

Classic—
Beautiful masterpiece.
The pianist bowed.
"Encore," the audience remarked.
Gifted hands producing magical music.

Ivan D. Villaluz | Philippines

Ivan D. Villaluz is a public school teacher, co-authored with his wife, Rosario Villaluz, their first book, *Semper Fi*, (*Always Faithful*). Ivan also contributed his poems to *Scentsibility, Anthology* under the GMGA Publishing banner.

COVID
(Change of Values, Introspection and Disposition)

Crown
Or Corona
Virus of mind
Impiety of the heart
Destruction of humanity at large

Crushes both soul and spirit
Omen foretold and prophesied
Vision of mystics
Inciting instructions
Divine

Crime
Of humanity
Vicious and venomous
Inflicting pain and death
Destruction of the human race

Change of character and heart
Open great positive possibilities
Values of men
Innate and
Divine

Earl Carlo Guevarra | Philippines

Earl Carlo Guevarra, is a 27-year-old proud Zamboangueño, and is an English teacher at a school in the heart of Manila. When he's not teaching, travelling, or drinking fruit shakes at home, he writes essays and poems.

New Normal

Times
have changed.
No huge
blowouts for us.
We hide behind masks.

Virtual birthdays,
distanced weddings,
parties of
old. Now
gone.

Death
is here.
A spectre
unseen, yet taints
our cherished moments.

Yet, plagues end. With
their passing comes
new life. Spring's
here to
stay.

Times
do change.
Let's shape new
paths and see the
sunrise together.

Naseha Sameen | India

Naseha Sameen was born in a town surrounded by two rivers and inhabited by people who celebrate in the face of natural calamity. It is a one-millennium old city, Cuttack. Silent starry nights, noisy cracking dawns, lazy afternoons loaded with champak odor, giggling evenings and early retreats of the day, all planted seeds of stories within her. After getting her Master's Degree, she moved to the bustling metropolis of Gurgaon where she crunched numbers and provided realistic strategies to corporates for a living. However, she knew she needed to tell a few stories. So started her writing journey. After fourteen years, she moved to Hyderabad, where she balances analytics and creative writing.

Anthology of poems, **Ruby Drops** is Amazon Best Seller in Poetry. The debut erotic political thriller **Heir: End of Innocence**, is a winner of Author Page awards for Best Debut and Best Woman Writer, Author of the Year - Inspiro Awards.

Untitled

Memories—
Unquenched thirst,
Ashes of dreams,
In vista of void
A twinkling warmth of hope.

In the realm of surreal
Piercing scream of pain
Inkling of completion,
Contended heart,
Memories!

Dreams—
Moist Lips,
Unfettered take off.
Soaring with amaranthine joy
On the grim time's lake

Stealing a smile from wrinkle
Of the worried brow
Moment of respite
In tribulation
Dreams!

Me
A collage
from moving kaleidoscope
Of dreams and memories,
Conflicts, contrasts, coherence and consonance

Mridusmita Choudhury | India

Mridusmita Choudhury is a writer, poet and entrepreneur from India. She has worked as a content writer for various organizations and also writes on her personal blogs. She has been passionately penning her thoughts and emotions since she was ten.

Her writings mainly talk about nature, philosophy, spirituality and human emotions. Many of her anecdotes and poetries connect inanimate nature with human behavior. She is a lover of poems that have natural rhymes but writes and reads free verse as well. Currently, she is working on her debut novel.

Messenger of my bloom

Messenger
Of my
Bloom planted some
Of his own into
My seedbed of million dreams.

I'd been a murky cloud
Ready to be touched
By another and
Create lives
Under.

I
Had been
A barren land
Craving to be drowned
Under a blissful venereal deluge.

Embraced my feeble chassis to
Create a cosmos within
And show me
My infinite
Power.

Created
Melody with
My restricted notes.
I'm a bloomed beauty.
My love, spring is here.

Amb Lovelyn P. Eyo | Nigeria

Amb Lovelyn P Eyo is a multi-award-winning poet from Nigeria. She is the Governor of Literary events and relationships with schools and universities for the World Union of Poets (Italy) and an administrator for the League of Poets (Nigeria). She is an International Ambassador for Peace & Cultural Creativity. India's Gujarat Government and Motivational Strips honored her with an award for excellence in literature at par with global standards on the occasion of India's 74th Independence Day. Lovelyn is also a recipient of the Tolerance medal for her contribution towards the culture of peace; International leadership noble award; 2020 World icon for peace and humanity, Global Humanitarian award; Shield of World Culture; Certificate of Merit by Kutai Mulawarman Kingdom of Indonesia, and many Gold Quills & Excellence awards for her poetic works. Her poems have been translated into Spanish, Efik, Bengali, Greek, Portuguese, and Chinese and also aired on *Radio America.*

SETS YOU FREE

Fear
Enfolds you
Inside of you
The gloomy butterfly hides
Will you ever be free?

When you let believe smile
The gloomy face changes
You only fly
Outside cocoons
High

Scared
Can't sing
Change comes knocking
You switch off light
Can you see the NEW?

Like the season changing cloaks
Old autumn gets disrobed
Winter sheds tears
Springing summer—
"Growth"

Florabelle Lutchman | Trinidad and Tobago

Mrs. **Florabelle Lutchman** is a retired principal. She has received many prestigious awards for her outstanding contribution to education. She has received awards from her church for her sterling contribution as an Elder and Local Board Secretary. She has written many papers for the *Presbyterian News*. She has also written many eulogies for her deceased loved ones. *Break the Silence* and *A Spark of Hope featured many of her poems*. She is a chief administrator in the sub forum "Poems Against Domestic Violence" of "How to Write for Success," and a member of "Motivational Strips".

She authored and co-authored the titles *Memories of a Teenager, Values for Life, Chaotic Times* and *A Husband Like Mine*

The Rescued Dog

Lucky
Her name
lived in sanctuary
Adopted twice by two
Sent back because of carelessness.

Sad
No home
Daughter was gone
As the blowing wind
Longing feelings overwhelmed mother dog.

Soon the same family appeared
Wishing for the mother
Quickly took her
Happily home
Met

Joy
Changed mannerisms
Happiness all around
Mother and daughter transformed
Living enjoying their dog years.

Aafiya Siddiqui | India

Aafiya Siddiqui who writes under the pen name aafiya_2, hails from Delhi, India. She enjoys penning her thoughts and endeavors to paint the canvas of life in shades of black and white with her poetic expressions. She has been a part of many poetry anthologies in Hindi and English including *Scentsibility*, *Psithurism*, *A Poet Was Born*, and *Rhapsodies*. You may follow her writings on Instagram scribbled_aafiyat.

POETRY

Golden sunrays singing
Aubade, planting a
Gentle kiss on cherubic
face of the sleeping carnations

Pearly Dew, dazzles and strews
Knocking on my window
Panes washing away
All the
Blues

Sillage
Of Shadows
Lingers in my
Heart, negating the
Resurrection of a new
morn, effacing rainbows of dreams

It's then, with cimmerian ink,
I Paint a Beamish
Sun smearing the
Pages with
Cordolium

Rp Verlaine | USA

Rp Verlaine lives and writes in New York City. He has an MFA in creative writing from City College. He taught in New York public schools for many years. Retired from teaching, he continues to write and do photography in New York. He had a volume of poetry *Damaged by Dames & Drinking* published in 2017 and *Femme Fatales Movie Starlets & Rockers* in 2018. A set of three e-books began with the publication of *Lies from The Autobiography Vol 1* in November of 2018. They published Vol 2 in 2019 and the third Volume in 2020.

His poetry has appeared in *Atlas Poetica, The Linnet's Wings, Chrysanthemum Literary Anthology, Last Stanza Poetry Journal, The Local Train, Proletaria, Haikuniverse, Scry of Lust 2 anthology, Rudderless Mariner, Humankind Journal, The Wild Word, Under The Basho, Plum Tree Tavern, Fresh Out Magazine, Scissortail Quarterly, Prune Juice, Incense Dreams, Best Poetry, Blazevox,* and *Pikers Press.*

Touched by Light

Nights
I become
A bird flying
Through the blind darkness
Always landing on God's shoulder

The church is my sanctuary
Praying only for myself
With no replies
But silence
Weeping.

Father
Handed me
His new rifle
I shot my first deer
"Becoming a man," he said.

The feel of a gun
All the frightened faces
I once saw
Robbing strangers
Friends.

Saved
In jail
By a light
Bright enough to blind
The evil in my soul.

Mary Eugene Flores | Philippines

Mary Eugene P. Flores is a graduate of Bachelor of Arts in English in Southern City Colleges, Zamboanga. She is a full-time data analyst-researcher and a freelance writer. She's currently managing a poetry page *"Life Is for Living, So Don't Sit at The Corner and Die."* The page currently gathered almost 5k followers as of this writing. As a Poet, she's personally interested in dark-speculative, narrative poetry, pieces that showing family struggle, her country's political, and social issues. She is a contributing writer of the books; *Voices of Aspirants: A collection of outstanding winning poets – 2016, Timeless Pieces of Scribbles – 2018*, and *Poetry Marathon Anthology – 2020.*

Young, Old

Cries,
At night,
A familiar light,
As mama cuddle's me,
Hums and let me sleep.

Those young old fragile memories,
A view from away,
A happy pill,
Was kept,
Here

Diminished,
Old light,
Mama's not here,
No more hums today,
Mama's from so far away.
A phone call once heard,
Your one last voice,
I hang up,
Cries hard,
Here

Emily Reid Green | USA

Emily Reid Green's poetry has appeared in various publications, including: *Gravel, Khroma Magazine, 1932 Quarterly, Moon Magazine,* and *The Ekphrastic Review.* Her first chapbook *Still Speak* was published in 2019 by Writing Knights Press. She has also been a sponsored poet with *Tiferet Journal* and their annual poem-a-thon. Emily lives in Toledo, Ohio with her family.

On Prayer

You
wring hands
expecting church bells—
Braided worry, sacred art
weaves tight across your knuckles.

Even a pin won't drop.
It knows ancient truth:
silence houses miracles,
tears unshed—
waiting.

Hold
your breath
only so long.
Sealed lapis lazuli lips,
blue that tilts toward heaven.

Seeking shelter from the storm
tomorrow's shadow softens, settles:
Under steepled fingers
a distant
thunder.

Kathy Jo (Blake) Bryant | USA

Kathy Jo (Blake) Bryant hails originally from Texas in the United States. She is now living in California. She is a Domestic Engineer, and an avid genealogist and a member of a lineage society. She has authored a two-volume book on genealogy. Even though she has written poetry intermittently from youth, she has had a positive surge in writing over the last couple of years after joining several poetry groups. Recently, she has had her poetry accepted on Bharath Vision, a top worldwide platform for writers and poets and The Sparrow, a recitative YouTube poetry group. She has received a growing number of poetry certificates of various kinds for Picture Prompts, and daily and weekly contests. *Open Door Poetry Magazine* featured a themed poem for their December issue, and they accepted three of her poems for an anthology coming up this spring.

Transformation

Music
Transforms us
Into new persons,
By relieving our stresses,
And completely overhauling our psyche.

Listening to good music soothes,
And releases our endorphins,
While causing relaxation.
Close eyelids,
Internalize.

Peaceful
Music calms
You and helps
You get great sleep,
So, you feel like working.

Listen closely with rapt attention,
To soft, lovely melodies,
Allowing them to
Transform you
Entirely!

Sharon Wagoner | USA

Sharon Wagoner's work frequently appears in *Jane Austen Magazine* and on Georgian Index.

The origins of words and objects in our lives have always fascinated her. They are like artifacts found in an archaeological dig. For example: ever wonder why we name the word for a meat and the animal it comes from differently, such as deer and venison? This dichotomy is because of the Norman Conquest in 1066. The Anglo-Saxon Serfs called the animal by a German name—deer, while the Norman Baron spoke French and called the roasted meat by the French word—venison.

Metamorphosis

Caterpillar,
Do you
Want to remain
On only one leaf
For all your short time?

You can make a change.
Put away the expected.
Imagine a better life.
Dream big.
Wings

Beautifully colored
Gliding the breezes
Truly are an option,
Butterfly, splendid and so free.

Flying everywhere is truly possible.
Build your exciting plan
You can be
A new
You.

When
That day,
Finally, is reached,
Metamorphosis has changed you.
It will be worth it!

Controversies
Humane realities,
Uncovering the mask,
Of malicious mental frugalities,
Causes more wreck than intended.

Spontaneous emission of metaphysical abruptions,
Cognition not under control,
Situation becomes critical,
Logical solution,
Transformation

Metamorphosis,
High-end resurrection
Sheathing your emotions
For stopping the outpour
Succumbing it inside a cocoon.

Transformation to a legendary achievement,
Without any physical obstructions,
Comes your way,
Profound happiness,
Heartiness.

Reinvigorate,
The innersole,
Joviality plays wonders,
Motivate yourselves, overcome disparities,
A reconstruction for self-embodiment

Karil Anand | India

She is a seasoned professional educator associated with a reputed school in Gurugram. Armed with a dynamic track record in career counselling, Karil Anand is value-driven and propelled by entrenched, benevolent principles. She shows striking calibre and tenacity through her feisty writings. Karil is an unparalleled literary quill who exhibits remarkable adeptness in semantics, as her pen spans across diverse genres both in Hindi and English. Karil presently partners with a renowned literature group—My Words: A Renaissance, as a moderator, and is an ardent contributor to literary journals. She has received many laurels and plaudits from social media for her writings.

Metamorphosis

Isolophilia
Repressive mind
In a false
sense of security clouds
Numbness drown me in despair.

Psychomachy
Defeated most
painful obstacles, ineffable
and scattered woebegone mind
Darkness holds the tight reins

Nepenthe
Being from
nothing can weave
Something masterful and artsy
To form a literary plethora.

Catharsis
Intellectual Synopsis
A literary bliss
From imaginative deepness
The metamorphosis of creative writing

Joel Trevor Saunders | Canada

Joel Trevor Saunders is from Ontario, Canada. He has been an avid reader and writer since he was a small boy and simply loves it.

Cycle

Pupa
Chrysalis wing
Transmuting cell mitosis
Compressed collected solid cocoons
Hung upon wood, dead alive

Predator meets prey hungers martyr
Pick peck motive lotus
Destinations much higher
Altitude feat
Flap

Rebirth
Grown new
Transform outer casing
Inside charged of fires
Spring human coated color butterflies

Break off carnivorous and free
Float in adversarial winds
Until wings give
Final thrusts
Death

Dipanjan Bhattacharjee | India

Dipanjan Bhattacharjee is an engineer by profession and a writer by passion. He completed his BTech in Electronics and Instrumentation Engineering in 2016. He has enjoyed literature since his school days. He has received over 430 certificates from various national and international literary communities and has also received titles such as Literary Colonel by StoryMirror and nominations from the International Book of Records for Longest Poem and Palindromic Poem.

Renaissance

Altruism!
Proffers serenity,
Through mortal world.
As beacon to darkness,
It kindles the divine flame.

Act of kindness reckons bliss,
Showering drops of elixir,
On suffering mankind.
Over time
Immemorial.

Perhaps,
This needs,
A noble heart,
And a pristine soul,
Brimmed with music of humanity.

Nurturing the roots of humanity,
With sunshine of thoughts,
Shall empower mankind,
With compassionate
Arms.

Renaissance,
Amid civilizations,
Requires inner thirst,
Brawny mind to initiate,
And explicit excogitation to perform.

The priceless gift of kindness,
As knights of time,
Must rule mankind,
With altruistic
Aura.

Imran Khan Bhayo | Pakistan

Imran Khan Bhayo is an author, editor, reader, and police officer. He is the author of three novels and one bestselling poetry book titled, *Poems Written Under my Grandfather's Tree*. Some of his poems have been published in magazines. He lives in a simple village called Karan Sharif, Sindh Province, Pakistan. He enjoys a life of reading and writing.

Untitled

Life twinkles like heaven's stars
If knowing heart's mysteries
Not in caves
But silent
Beauty

Beauty
Not magic
But natural logic
Always brightens every corner
With beautiful and spiritual colours

Colours' clouds flying like birds
Flowing like roaring rivers
Shower blessing drops
For thirsty
Earth

Earth
Loves all
Humans and animals
Birds and insects living
In it or on it

It is the beautiful pronoun
Use instead of noun
Beautifying both subject
And object
Palaces

Palaces
Are built
With previous stones
Erecting the golden pillars
In deserts and on mountains
Mountains cry with Hellenic tears

Flowing like flooding oceans
Burning and ruining
Swallowing everything
Everlasting

Everlasting
Mirrors are
The Natural truths
Obeying, following and blooming
But don't disobey like humans

Humans' spiritual way is truth
Knowing everything but wander
Seeing prophetic miracles
Deny own
Wisdom

Wisdom
Perennially lives
In heart's garden
With magical roses' pleasures
Awakening subconscious mind of life

David Wagoner | USA

David Wagoner is a retired CAD-CAM programmer and shop manager of precision parts and 3-D printing. His greatest thrill was to work on parts that went into space, including several parts for The Space Shuttle. He is also interested in poetry and writing. His father was an engineer and his mother an English teacher. He has had poems in Spillwords and Raven's Cage and published a poetry book *Scratches on Scraps,* and edited the anthology *A Promise of Doves.*

Metaphorphosis

Choose
To be
The one who
Lays the steps up
To your very best self!

Begin with small doable steps.
Celebrate each you achieve.
Map the way
Building always
Toward ...

You
Will emerge
At the top
Of those arduous steps
As a far better you!

Andrew Geoffrey Kwabena Moss

Andrew Geoffrey Kwabena Moss is a writer and teacher who has lived in the UK, Japan and currently Australia. Of Anglo-Ghanaian heritage, his work seeks to explore and challenge liminal landscapes, complex identities and the social constructs of race. Andrew is a member of the ACT Writers' Centre and has previously had work published by Afropean, People in Harmony, Fly on the Wall Press and The Word Bin podcast.

Anansi Transformations

Anansesem*
Captivating narratives
From Sky-God Onyamekopon
Spanning sea mouths, word
capturing spider stories for eternity

Bridge thread across Atlantic seas
Single strand, tensile strength
Spider Weaver of
change, continuity
Anansi

Looming
Pattern shifting
Taking story shapes
Transatlantic transformations spanning nations
Stitching silky kente, super-strength specialisation

Captivity transcending, time and space
Metamorphosing, asserting boundaried identities
Trickster turning tables
Plantation Tactics
Survival

Anansi
Akan uncanny
Spider weaving trickster
Spinning survival stories gracefully
Transforming transatlantic slavery gloriously.

*The term Anansesem refers to the storytelling tradition of the
Akan-speaking people of West Africa. The word, when translated
to English, means "Ananse stories" or "Spider
tales." Anansesem encompasses the performative art of
storytelling associated with Ananse, "the Spider," in the Twi
dialect of Akan.

Anna Maria Dall'Olio | Italy

MA Languages: English and Portuguese, BA Italian Letters. She has been teaching English in Italian high schools since 1987. She devoted herself to poetry, fiction and playwriting. In 2005 she was ranked second in *"Hanojo - via Rendevuo"*, a Vietnamese cultural competition for the millennial celebration of Hanoj (1010-2010). Moreover, she was ranked first/second/third in lots of literary competitions for her Italian poems (2006-2018).

She published a novel, *"Segreti"* (2018) as well as 5 collections of poems in Italian: *"Sì shabby chic"* (2018), *"L'acqua opprime"*; (2016), *"Fruttorto sperimentale"* (2016), *"Latte & Limoni"* (2014), *"L'angoscia del pane"*; (2010). She also wrote 2 plays: *"Evoluzioni"* (2019) and its Esperanto prequel *"Tabelo"*; (2006) dealing with mobbing as a supreme artistic form.

Something new

Such hard years of toil
changed your hard cocoon:
no more caterpillar,
some more
butterfly.

Unfurl
your wings
dare to fly
go with the wind
show off your own colors.

Never have you felt alive
whatever vessel you used
yours is overflowing
hiding something
new.

You,
bright example
brimming with life,
are somebody else's story
in different places, different times.

Arundhati Mukherjee | India

Arundhati Mukherjee is an engineer by profession and writer, author, blogger, poet and singer by passion. She is the deputy chief engineer in a thermal power plant. She writes in Speaking Tree, Times of India initiative, and author in e-magazines like *Pragyata*, Thrive Global and Sivana East. Recently she had self-published a poetry book through Amazon KDP, *Bohemian Rhapsody: A Travelers Musings Through The Journey Of Life*, the foreword of which was written by eminent poetess and moderator of Motivational Strips, Vandana Sudeesh. The paperback version is being processed and will be published soon. She is an active member of the world's most active writer's forum, Motivational Strips.

LOVE TRANSFORMS

I
drifted about
Hither and thither
Lonely amidst crowd unknown,
Life alleys disintegrated true self.

Lost in the vicissitudes of life,
I pined for solace,
Peace , untwined
Soul.

Love
Appeared suddenly
Tearing apart stupendously,
Veil of ignorance surreptitiously,
Thus, integrating the universe progressively.

The selfish egocentric ruthless I,
Transformed to pure we,
As heart opened
Light entered
Divinely.

Metamorphosis of ego consciousness happened,
The shell fell apart,
Self-spread wings,
True self
Shines

Sakina Mohammed | Sri Lanka

Sakina Mohammed is a Sri Lankan poet, a professional Henna artist, and a full-time mother. She actively publishes her spoken and written poetry on her Instagram page www.instagram.com@sakinas_expressions on the themes of emotional and mental well-being, life realities and motivational subjects. Motivational Strips, The World's Most Active Writer's Forum appointed Sakina as a moderator of their literary forum. They have also featured her multiple times on the Bharat Vision website, which is affiliated with the Motivational Strips Forum. She was on the inaugural episode, as well as the upcoming first episode for the Bharat Vision Channel, also affiliated to the Motivational Strips Forum. Eve Poetry Magazine website nominated her as the Poet of the Day. The Union Hispanomundial De Escritores

(UHE), the world's largest Spanish Writers Union, awarded her the 'Cesar Vallejo 2020' award. Currently she is working on her upcoming book *MY POETIC PLACE: The Journey to Self-Discovery.*

ROSEN POTENTIAL!

Red,
Blossoming buds ...
Prepared for transformation
Into magnificent fragrant roses ...
All destined for matured flourish!

Heartbreaking some buds wont bloom,
Some not flourish prime ...
Leaving landscaper retrospecting
Possible reasons ...
Contemplating!!!

Why?
Does ponder
Disturbed, hurt landscaper—
Deep evaluation would answer
The cause of uneven growth!

Sun light ceased to befall
Upon the few cornered
Half bloomed roses—
Hits hard
Realization!

Transformation
Genuinely occurs
When positive illumination
Is allowed within individuals—
Surrounded by darkness, growth halts!!

To bloom with highest potential,
Become our best versions ...
Each should SEEK
And ACCEPT
LIGHT!

Steven Webb | United Kingdom

Steven was born in England in 1961 and moved to South Africa with his parents in 1971. After completing his schooling, he joined the military and thereafter the Emergency Services where he became an Advanced Life Support paramedic. He now assists authors around the world in achieving their dreams by ensuring their manuscripts receive the attention they deserve. Steven is the author of four books, including the bestselling title, *Midnight in Ndola*.

The Challenge

Author, trying to write something
Blank pages stare back
A challenge set
The winner,
Unknown

Author
Stares back
The challenge accepted
The writing is complete,
The author becomes the winner

Perwaiz Shaharyar | India

Dr. Perwaiz Shaharyar is an editor of the National Council of Educational Research and Training (NCERT), Ministry of Education, Government of India. He was also the Principal Publication Officer in National Council for Promotion of Urdu Language in 2007. He is a famous short story writer, poet, and critic from India. He graduated with English Honors from Ranchi University.

Sun
Moon, stars
All are moving
Around my sleeping beloved
The center of my universe!

My beloved is the center
My heart does pivot
Where she stands
Holding my
Hands

Aine S. Losauro | Philippines

Aine Albancis Losauro is a wife, a mother, and an OFW in Singapore. She co-authored the book *Bards from The Far East: Anthology of Haiku and Kindred Verses* along with four multi-awarded poets namely Ayo Gutierrez, Felix Fojas, Jose Rizal M. Reyes, and Danny Gallardo. She writes poetry to appease herself from loneliness away from home under the pseudonym of "Ligaw Makata. She writes her poems in English, Filipino and Hiligaynon. She is also one of the translators of *The Gift* by Luzviminda Gabato Rivera which she translated into Hiligaynon.

Deep Well of Melancholy

Rest
your mind
down the deep-
well of soulful melancholy
dwelling the pace of recollection.

Keep your stillness in rejuvenation.
Once you've settled calmly,
Find your way
Slowly to
Relinquish

the
fire burning
feeling inside you
not wanting to extinguish,
but to be recognized freely

by the time of mercy.
when charity of heart
pours out to comfort
your remorseful
soul,

you'll
live again.
Arose from the
deep well of melancholy
newly baptized in January rain.

Sreekala P. Vijayan | India

Sreekala P. Vijayan is an award-winning poet by passion and academician by profession. She started writing since her school days. She is a moderator of Motivational Strips, the world's most active writer's forum and listed member of World Nations Writer's Union. She authored a bestselling poetry book titled *Soul in Whole*.

Untitled

Controversies
Humane realities,
Uncovering the mask,
Of malicious mental frugalities,
Causes more wreck than intended.

Spontaneous emission of metaphysical abruptions,
Cognition not under control,
Situation becomes critical,
Logical solution,
Transformation

Metamorphosis,
High-end resurrection
Sheathing your emotions
For stopping the outpour
Succumbing it inside a cocoon.

Transformation to a legendary achievement,
Without any physical obstructions,
Comes your way,
Profound happiness,
Heartiness.

Reinvigorate,
The innersole,
Joviality plays wonders,
Motivate yourselves, overcome disparities,
A reconstruction for self-embodiment

Dale Brendan Hyde | United Kingdom

Dale Brendan Hyde was born in Salford Hope Hospital in 1974. He has lived apart from spells in the Middle East & Norway mostly in his Mother's home city of Wakefield. He published his first poetry book by Route at the Yorkshire Art circus for the prestigious T.S. Elliot prize. Dale is the author of the bestselling titles *The Whiskey Pool, The Gods R Watchin, The Ink Run,* & *Stitched.*

Metaphorphosis

Broken
Hopeful fracture
Pains long remembered
Swathed in Crystal bandage
Cocooned beyond life's brutal reach

Mended in the eyes blink
Knitted back together stronger
Scars show mapped
Upon highways
Journey

Healed
Blissful rapture
Scar tissue still
Pulling inside like heart
Yanking me to recall retreat

Poetry Campers

This section features young and upcoming poets from the poetry camp initiated by GMGA Publishing.

and
they pen
their paths leaving
sight trails sketching maps
of vision. roads stretch. Witness

steps at daybreak. when their
ballpoints highway to noon's
rise, they'll reach
their mission's
sun.
-db

Danielle Q. Patalinghug

Danielle Q. Patalinghug is 10 years old. She loves reading books and writing poems. Her favorite forms of poetry are haiku and tan(g)ka.

What Matters Most

Friendship,
Precious jewel,
Hard to find,
A friend in deed,
Is a friend to me.

Dinah Lourence P. Boiser

Dinah Lourence P. Boiser, 15, is an incoming 9th grader at Living Stones International School. She plays volleyball, basketball, the guitar, and loves books, especially those of Rick Riordan and Nicholas Sparks. Her favorite subjects include Social Studies, Speech and Journalism, and Science. She was given the opportunity to learn and train under GMGA Publishing's poetry camp, headed by Coach Ayo, to practice different forms of poetry. Her most favorite forms of poetry are haiku and rhyming poems.

Changes in Time

People change as seasons do
Memories made and gone
Friends, foes, families
All changing
Slowly

Construct of Love

Love
Takes time
To fully accept
You and your mistakes
Forever, through thick and thin

Ydrianne Luz S. Castor

Ydrianne Luz S. Castor is a Business Management graduate and just started her career in government service. Aside from scribbling poems and drawing, she also loves cartoon movies. She hopes to compile her collection of poems someday.

Untitled

Heart
Two ears
One body soul
Conceive distinct possible emotions
In love and bitterness sweet

Frightening it may be but
Once convalescence appears within
Everything fades then
Felicity commences
Suddenly.

Raphaelle Marie B. Villaluz

Raphaelle Marie B. Villaluz, is the daughter of Ivan and Rosario Villaluz, authors of the poetry book, *Semper Fi*. Aside from writing poems and short stories, Raphaelle also plays the flute, guitar, and ukulele and dances like a bumblebee. She is a Grade 7 student under the Special Science Curriculum, and her love for various languages inspired her to work as foreign service officer in the future.

For Keeps

Love
Without counting
Its great cost
Is the kind of
Love worth keeping for constantly

Liane Gabrielle B. Villaluz

Liane Gabrielle B. Villaluz, 14, is a Grade 9 student under the Special Science Curriculum. She is the eldest daughter of Ivan and Rosario Villaluz, authors of the poetry book, *Semper Fi*. Aside from writing poems, Liane also plays the violin, piano, guitar and ukulele, and wants to become a pediatrician in the future. She has enrolled in two poetry writing camps conducted by GMGA Publishing to hone her poetry writing skills.

Eternal Ties

Family
Bonded strongly
Cannot be separated
Even when storms come
They just become even stronger

Viktoriah Simonne A. Verano

Viktoriah Simonne Verano, 13, is a Grade 7 student. Her hobbies include arts and crafts, playing board games, reading books, and writing journals. She takes interest in flower gardening, science, and history. One of her life's goals is to publish her artwork and stories.

Friendship

Friends
Are significant
Like a treasure
That everyone wants,
Do you have any friends?

Being with them is fun!
Lots of memories keep
happening with an
album stores
everything.

Alexandreah Louisse A. Verano

Alexandreah Louisse A. Verano is a grade 7 student from Lapu-Lapu City, Cebu. During this Covid time, she spends her quarantine days pursuing her love for arts like doodling, watercolor painting, and learning more about digital art. In between school modules and house chores, she also reads books and writes stories and poems. Writing and publishing her artwork are two of her life goals.

Gratitude

Thanks
for all
the memories that
I hold so dearly
In my heart. I'm grateful

You are there for me
You are lovely like
the daisy flowers
that bloom
kindness.

Alexa G. Abanggan

Alexa is a Grade 3 student. She loves writing, digital art, music, and Math. She loves to go to the beach with her family. Her dream is to become a gynecologist.

My Treasures

I
Cherish my
Family, pets, friends
Because they care unconditionally
They remain true and steadfast

Carlos G. Abanggan

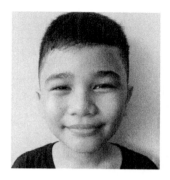

Carlos is an 11-year-old author. He loves drawing as a hobby, and his favorite food is chicken. He loves to invest in the stock market with his dad, invents things, try out new recipes with his mom, and play with his three younger sisters. His favorite insect is the ant; his dream is to build an ant-themed park in the future. He plans to study Robotics in Japan. He also wants to witness snow. He wants to be an illustrator, author, and entomologist.

Nature's Irony

Trees
Blocking elements
From strong disasters
Sadness, into burning ashes
Such cruelty in this world

Maria Antonia E. Barandog

Maria Antonia E. Barandog works as a staff in a public senior high school in Negros Oriental, Philippines. Inspired by other poets/authors who started inking their legacy in their middle ages, she just started hers through the tutelage of best-selling author and book coach, Ayo Gutierrez. It has been her desire to share her stories, experiences, and thoughts in life through poetry and prose.

Untitled

Alone
In battle
That inflicts my
Corporal and mental health
Spare me from your severity

For I am totally feeble
No! You can't claim
Victory over me!
God loves
Me

Dinah Beatrice N. Villegas

Dinah Beatrice N. Villegas is a Grade 6 student at Banilad Elementary School. Her favorite subjects are Math and Science. She has two younger sisters and one older sister. She also loves to play piano, guitar, and ukulele. She plans to be a chef in the future.

I'm
So lucky
To have you
As my best friend,
I love you so much

Denize Ynah Ruth N. Villegas

Denize Ynah Ruth N. Villegas is a Grade 7 student from Talamban High School. She has three younger sisters. She loves to read books and learn music. She enjoys beach outings with her family and loves to eat ice cream for dessert. She is also an aspiring writer and a filmmaker.

Aking Sinta

Ang
Iyong alaala
Ay tila bago
Na sa aking panaginip
Dumudungaw at hindi mawala-wala.

Siguro nga, matatawa ka kung
alam mo ang nadarama ko
para sa'yo na
kay hirap
panindigan.

Ngunit..

Dumaan
Man ang
Hirap at pasakit,
Ikaw pa rin ang
Tangi kong mamahalin, aking sinta.

Magbago man ang ating mundo,
Mamahalin pa rin kita
Nang buong puso
Ngayon at
Magpakailanman.

My Dear

Memories
Of you
Are somewhat new.
These memories visit me
In my dreams and stay.

Maybe you'd find it funny
To know my feelings
For you that
I couldn't
Admit.

Though
Problems and
Pain may come,
It is you alone
I will love, My Dear.

Though our world keeps changing,
I will love you
Truly always, Dear,
Now and
Forever.

-translation by LS

Asianne Zuleika T. Fernandez

Asianne Zuleika T. Fernandez, aka AZ, is a nine-year-old girl. She is the oldest among five siblings. Her many interests include baking, singing, dancing, writing, planning parties, create movies, sew, and design. She is good in Science and English.

Summer

We
Meet at
The beach, so
Nice and free. Summer
Breeze. Water splashes. Sand castles.

Oh, the sun is setting.
Yes! We gotta go
See you next
Time. Do
Great!

Closing

We sincerely hope that you have enjoyed reading and musing on the varied shades and layers of "metaphorphosis" presented in this collection. GMGA Publishing is committed in paving the way for births and transformations in the literary world. We exist to help you "ink your legacy". Visit www.inkyourlegacy.com and email gmgapublishing@gmail.com for your publishing needs.

when
voices rest
as the breeze
weaves waves and ripples
among the leaves of seas,

new breaths will grow oceans
and versespeak tree tides...
seed...swim...sail...
transcend...transfigure...
transform...
-db

ABOUT THE ARTIST

Jinque RD is an award-winning international poet, Amazon bestseller author, graphic designer, novelist, and a well-known book illustrator. She is based in Palauig, Zambales, Philippines and has designed and illustrated great number of books for authors across the globe while taking pride in promoting sustainable living and allowing herself to be a free spirit who continually wants to evolve in her best version.

References

Lodge, Angela. (August 2020) Author Biography, Retrieved from Spillwords – A place for readers and writers, where Words Matter website: https://spillwords.com

Dall'Olio, Anna Maria. (November 2019) Author Biography. Retrieved from Sahitto Bilingual Literary Magazine website: https://sahitto.com

Verlaine, RP. Author Biography. Retrieved from RP Verlaine Poetry website: https://thewildword.com/

Lisa Tomey (Host) (October 2020) Prolific Pulse Poetry Podcast. Bryant, Kathy Jo (Blake). Anchor by Spotify. https://anchor.fm

Siddiqui, Aafiya. Biography. Retrieved from Eve Poetry Magazine website: https://evepoetry.com/

Sameen, Naseha. Biography. Retrieved from goodreads website: https://www.goodreads.com/ accessed 4/24/2021

Guevarra, Earl Carlo. Biography. Retrieved from Dreamslayer website: https://www.dreamslayer28.com

Magpile, Christine Marie Lim. Biography. Retrieved form Philippine Literature Portal website: https://panitikan.ph/

Rekha, Srivalli. Biography. Retrieved from goodreads website: https://www.goodreads.com

Ahmed, Sarfraz. Biography. Retrieved from Green Cat books website: https://www.green-cat.co/safraqz-ahmed

Lodge, Andrea. (August 2020) Biography. Retrieved from Spillwords – A place for readers and writers, where Words Matter website: https://www.spillwords.com/ranunculus/

Guardiola-Lopez, Karina. Biography. Retrieved from KG Lopez website: www.kglopez.com

Willitts, Martin Jr. (October 2020) Biography. Retrieved from Poets and Writers 50 and forward website: https://www.pw.org/

Santiago, Ernesto P. (November 2017) Biography. Retrieved from Iwa Bogdani, International Writers Association website: https://www.iwabogdani.org/

Ganguli, Ipsita. (March 2021) Biography. Retrieved from the Setu website: https://www.setumag.com

Shankar Amit. Biography. Retrieved from Wikipedia website: https://en.wikipedia.org

Printed in Great Britain
by Amazon

62710043R00169